MICROCOMPUTERS FOR PROCESS CONTROL

NOTICE TO READERS

Dear Reader

An Invitation to Publish in and Recommend the Placing of a Standing Order to Volumes Published in this Valuable Series

If your library is not already a standing/continuation order customer to this series, may we recommend that you place a standing/continuation order to receive immediately upon publication all new volumes. Should you find that these volumes no longer serve your needs, your order can be cancelled at any time without notice.

The Editors and the Publisher will be glad to receive suggestions or outlines of suitable titles, reviews or symposia for editorial consideration: if found acceptable, rapid publication is guaranteed.

ROBERT MAXWELL
Publisher at Pergamon Press

MICROCOMPUTERS FOR PROCESS CONTROL

R. C. HOLLAND, B.Sc., M.Sc.

West Glamorgan Institute of Higher Education, Swansea, Wales

PERGAMON PRESS

OXFORD · NEW YORK · TORONTO · SYDNEY · PARIS · FRANKFURT

U.K.	Pergamon Press Ltd., Headington Hill Hall, Oxford OX3 0BW, England
U.S.A.	Pergamon Press Inc., Maxwell House, Fairview Park, Elmsford, New York 10523, U.S.A.
CANADA	Pergamon Press Canada Ltd., Suite 104, 150 Consumers Road, Willowdale, Ontario M2J 1P9, Canada
AUSTRALIA	Pergamon Press (Aust.) Pty. Ltd., P.O. Box 544, Potts Point, N.S.W. 2011, Australia
FRANCE	Pergamon Press SARL, 24 rue des Ecoles, 75240 Paris, Cedex 05, France
FEDERAL REPUBLIC OF GERMANY	Pergamon Press GmbH, Hammerweg 6, D-6242 Kronberg-Taunus, Federal Republic of Germany

First edition 1983

Library of Congress Cataloging in Publication Data
Holland, R. C.
 Microcomputers for process control.
 (Materials engineering practice)
 Includes index.
 1. Process control — Data processing.
 2. Microcomputers. I Title. II. Series.
TS156.8.H65 1983 629.8'028'54 82-12236

British Library Cataloguing in Publication Data
Holland, R.C.
Microcomputers for process control.—(Materials engineering practice)
1. Process control—Data processing
2. Microcomputer systems
I. Title II. Series
670.42'7   TS156.8
ISBN 0-08-029957-1 (Hardcover)
ISBN 0-08-029956-3 (Flexicover)

Printed in Great Britain by A. Wheaton & Co. Ltd., Exeter

Materials Engineering Practice

FOREWORD

The title of this new series of books "Materials Engineering Practice" is well chosen since it brings to our attention that in an era where science, technology and engineering condition our material standards of living, the effectiveness of practical skills in translating concepts and designs from the imagination or drawing board to commercial reality, is the ultimate test by which an industrial economy succeeds.

The economic wealth of this country is based principally upon the transformation and manipulation of *materials* through *engineering practice*. Every material, metals and their alloys and the vast range of ceramics and polymers has characteristics which requires specialist knowledge to get the best out of them in practice, and this series is intended to offer a distillation of the best practices based on increasing understanding of the subtleties of material properties and behaviour and on improving experience internationally. Thus the series covers or will cover such diverse areas of practical interest as surface treatments, joining methods, process practices, inspection techniques and many other features concerned with materials engineering.

It is to be hoped that the reader will use this book as the base on which to develop his own excellence and perhaps his own practices as a result of his experience and that these personal developments will find their way into later editions for future readers. In past years it may well have been true that if a man made a better mousetrap the world would beat a path to his door. Today however to make a better mousetrap requires more direct communication between those who know how to make the better mousetrap and those who wish to know. Hopefully this series will make its contribution towards improving these exchanges.

MONTY FINNISTON

Preface

A large range of textbooks have been published recently to satisfy the demand for explanations of the new microprocessor technology. These books generally have concentrated on logic design and microprocessor operation. They are particularly helpful to microcomputer system designers, programmers and hobbyists.

This book is aimed at practising engineers in industry who wish to acquire a base of understanding of this technology and also to learn how microcomputers can actually be applied in real plant situations. Considerable emphasis is given to plant measurements, interfacing techniques and applications of microcomputers for plant monitoring and control.

No prior knowledge of microprocessor technology is assumed, but some awareness of plant measurement and control problems will assist the reader. Students undertaking engineering courses which include microelectronics or process control studies should find the text helpful.

The position of the microcomputer in the computer hierarchy is very clearly that of the newcomer which is far smaller and cheaper than its predecessors but also far less powerful. The mainframe computer, which can cost more than £1,000,000 handles enormous data filing and multi-user systems, e.g. large service industry customer accounts, factory payroll and invoicing, Police filing system, etc. The minicomputer is smaller and can cost from £5,000 to £200,000. It is used for process control, smaller information handling systems and as terminals for mainframe computers. The microcomputer can cost from £5 to £15,000 and it has brought cheap computing in many forms to every consumer. Applications in the home, office and factory are described in this book. The main emphasis however is on techniques for process monitoring and control.

Contents

Chapter 1

Survey of Microprocessor Applications

1.1 INTRODUCTION

The advent of the digital computer in the 1960s was described at the time as the second Industrial Revolution. It was predicted that traditional job patterns, business and industrial activity and even the individual's social and leisure activities would be totally transformed. This feared absorption of the individual has only occurred to a minor degree in the intervening period.

The computer did replace a large proportion of clerical and administrative jobs. Scientific and process-control functions were assisted by the applications of computers. However, large-scale unemployment has not been caused directly by computer-based filing and control systems. Other causes have precipitated escalating unemployment since the late 1970s and in any case the computer industry has generated its own jobs. Whilst many computer systems performed useful and cost-effective functions, many mistakes were made in computer-system design and inappropriate application by enthusiastic computer "buffs" and eager but bewildered factory and business managers who felt technologically naked without their quota of these new machines. The dubious cost-effectiveness of many systems has never been analysed.

One wonders whether the euphoric reception of the new computer—the microprocessor—by the media, the electronics/computer industry and government departments is similarly exaggerated. There are two reasons why on this occasion the predictions may approach reality more closely:

(a) Cost—the microprocessor is so cheap.
(b) The track record of the microprocessor—the scale of its application within the last few years has been staggering.

A medium-power microprocessor in its silicon-chip form can be bought for less than £10. A handful of additional less complex chips enable a complete microcomputer to be built. This microcomputer can match the computing power of conventional digital computers which were housed in several large cubicles. A single chip microcomputer which comprises low-power microprocessor plus auxiliary circuitry can be manufactured in Third World countries for application in digital watches, video games and pocket calculators for perhaps £2 to £4. The cost reductions due to mass production have been impressive. The first digital watch was marketed at over £300. These products can now be bought for less than £10. For these reasons the microprocessor represents a major advance in technology and economic application.

1.2 MASS-PRODUCED CONSUMER DEVICES

By far the most numerous applications of the microprocessor have been in the everyday consumer products of digital watches, pocket calculators and video games. In these cases the microprocessor is invariably 4-bit (compared with the later more powerful 8-bit or 16-bit microprocessors) and includes memory and input/output circuitry on the same chip. A battery and display device complete the unit. The following descriptions apply to these systems:

1.2.1 Digital watch (see Figure 1.1)

The microcomputer in its single-chip form is critically time controlled by a crystal clock. It continuously updates the liquid crystal display with the date or time or whatever other function is selected. This type of display is exceptionally low powered and makes little demand on the battery. As the microcomputer program increments its time count it is also updating each 7-segment digit display in turn.

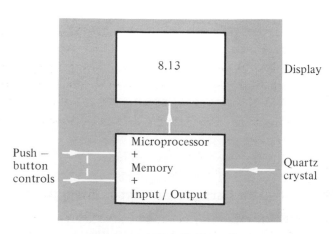

FIGURE 1.1 DIGITAL WATCH

1.2.2 Pocket calculator (see Figure 1.2)

In this case the keyboard requires a much larger number of input signals and a second chip often handles the display and keyboard input/output requirements. Again the liquid crystal display, LCD, has largely replaced the LED (light-emitting diode) display because of power requirements. The microcomputer program can become considerably longer and more complex for calculators with extensive scientific, trigonometric and statistical functions and for those which can be partially programmed by the operator.

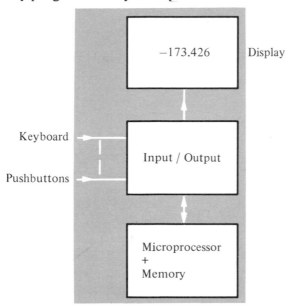

FIGURE 1.2 POCKET CALCULATOR

1.2.3 Video games (see Figure 1.3)

In this case the microcomputer includes an additional chip which generates a normal television signal (vision modulated on UHF carrier). The microcomputer program draws the playing area boundaries on the television screen and superimposes on this the dynamic game ball. The operator's game controls, or "paddles", are potentiometers which control simple timing circuits which the program reads.

Other applications which are becoming commonplace but which are mass-produced at a much lower level are as follows:

1.2.4 Petrol-pump control (see Figure 1.4)

Unreliable mechanical integrators and display devices have been replaced by a PCB (printed circuit board) holding a small number of chips. The microcomputer drives 7-segment LED displays to produce bright indication of petrol quantity and price.

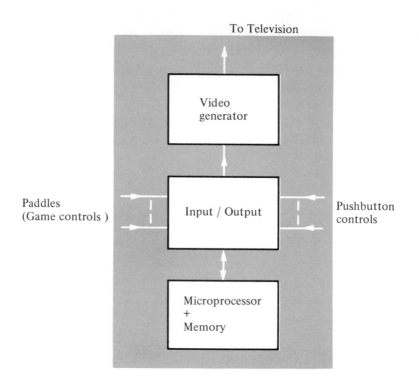

FIGURE 1.3 VIDEO GAME

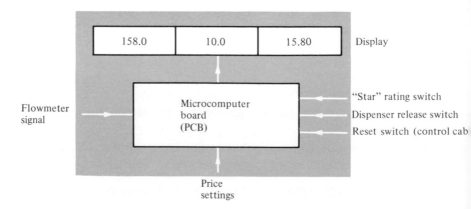

FIGURE 1.4 PETROL PUMP CONTROLLER

1.2.5 Washing-machine controller (see Figure 1.5)

The microcomputer represents an ideal application for the replacement of a complex mechanical timing and sequence control mechanism by a compact, reliable and low-cost alternative.

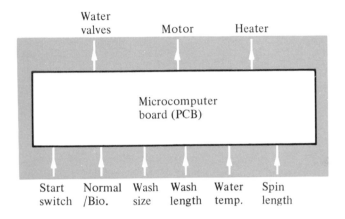

FIGURE 1.5 WASHING MACHINE CONTROLLER (& TIMER)

1.2.6 Cash register

This is simply a heavy-duty equivalent of the calculator. However, microcomputer cash registers can now be linked to more powerful computers which perform stock control and automatic re-ordering. In some American stores automatic debiting of the customer's bank account is carried out.

1.2.7 Fruit machine

A random (?) number generator program drives stepper motors to show the luckless punter how commercially biased some computer programs can be.

1.2.8 Miscellaneous additional products

Such as toys and games (although be warned that computer chess "masters" can apparently seldom stretch a good club player!)

Clearly a summarising list such as this is not comprehensive and will be expanded rapidly in time when untapped applications become exploited.

1.3 COMMERCIAL SYSTEMS

Microcomputers have made substantial inroads into the office. The principal areas of application are as follows:

1.3.1 The desktop computer for microcomputer-based information filing systems

A typical assembly is shown in Figure 1.6. The operator communicates to the computer via a typewriter style of keyboard. A small CRT, or Cathode Ray Tube (typically 10 in. to 14 in. in screen size) displays the information entered and requested by the operator. A floppy-disc drive unit is included for bulk storage of information and programs.

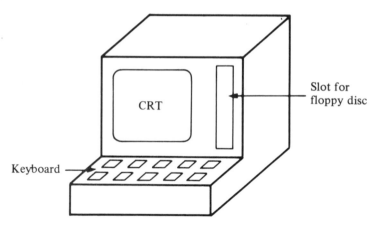

FIGURE 1.6 DESKTOP COMPUTER ASSEMBLY

Sometimes a printer is added to the configuration in order to produce a hard copy of data stored, data entered and data calculated when required by the operator. The block schematic of such a system could then look like Figure 1.7.

Such systems sell for prices from a few hundred pounds to a few thousand pounds. Competition from the several manufacturers is intense and each manufacturer supports his equipment with a wide range of administrative and accounting functions which are held as programs on floppy disc as follows:

PAYROLL—suitable for small organisation of a few hundred employees or less.

PURCHASE/SALES LEDGER—comprehensive records can be held on file and updated by the operator.

STOCK CONTROL—as above.

SPECIALISED FILING SYSTEMS—e.g. mailing list, personnel file, estate agency property file, etc.

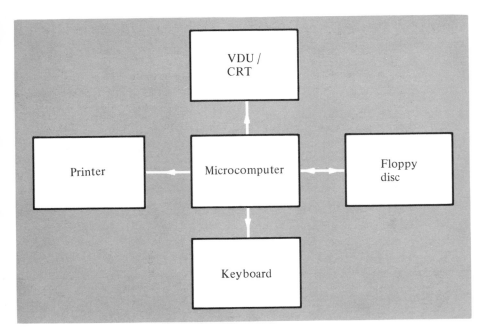

FIGURE 1.7 DESKTOP COMPUTER BLOCK SCHEMATIC

1.3.2 The word processor

Sometimes a word-processor-program function is offered with a generalised desktop computer system as just described. More flexible and powerful word processors are built as single-function microcomputer configurations.

The word processor operates as an aid to the typist. In fact it represents one of the most fundamental changes in job pattern for any of the microcomputer applications. The typist still operates a typewriter keyboard but, in place of direct production of hard copy print, the entered text is stored within the microcomputer's memory and displayed on a VDU (Visual Display Unit) screen. This enables the operator to perform highly flexible editing of the text, e.g. insertion and deletion of words/lines/paragraphs and block insertion of previously entered text. Clearly this latter feature is of considerable benefit when standard letter or report text blocks are repeated in many different document types, e.g. letter headings, repetitive paragraphs in legal documents, conditions of sale, etc.

When the typist/operator has completed entry and editing, he/she calls the print facility and the computer produces a precise page-formatted copy on its printer. Whilst the computer is producing a multi-page printout the operator can commence entry and editing of a separate document.

1.3.3 Multi-computer network

A microcomputer terminal can form part of a "Distributed Processing System". Such a system is shown in Figure 1.8. The various processing functions are segregated into different machines in the network. The machines are often in different locations. Communication links between machines enable data to be passed around the network.

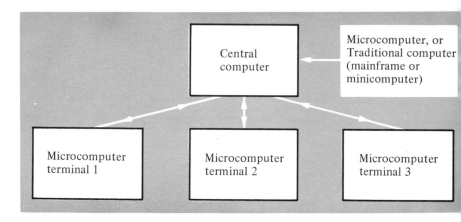

FIGURE 1.8 DISTRIBUTED PROCESSING SYSTEM

A microcomputer terminal in such a network can possess the business functions which are available in the desktop computer described in section 1.3.1 above, plus the communications feature which enables information and program facility access to other parts of the network. Whilst a straightforward desktop computer can cost less than £1000 more powerful computers which are designed as terminals in such an application cost a few thousand pounds.

1.4 FACTORY APPLICATIONS

Applications for process monitoring and control form the main content of this book. However, a brief summary of the principal application areas is as follows:

1.4.1 Plant logging and control

Figure 1.9 shows a simplified representation of a microcomputer applied to a plant monitoring and control function. The system may not have a VDU if a straightforward control function is required but data display to operators is not required. Such an application may be a sequence control system or an instrumentation, e.g. gas analyser, control task.

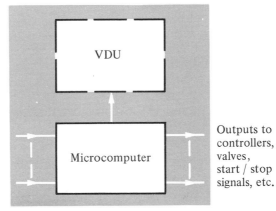

FIGURE 1.9 PLANT CONTROL APPLICATION

A VDU will be added if plant information is to be presented to the operator or if access is required to the computer's database, e.g. instrumentation readings or plant state, for diagnostic purposes by maintenance personnel. Such systems are often highly customised, i.e. they are configured and programmed for specific functions.

The range of such applications is extremely diverse. Examples are:

BATCH CONTROL of processes.

INSTRUMENTATION LOGGING AND CALIBRATION which may include computer program linearising of non-linear instrument readings, combination of several readings in calculation procedures, alarm checking and anunciation, etc.

PLANT START-UP/SHUTDOWN in sequence control systems.

WEIGHING CONTROL perhaps including auto-taring, self-calibration, displays driving and data transmission to other machines and many more.

A simple maxim for such applications is that if a control or logging requirement exists and an electrical interface can be created, then a microcomputer provides a flexible, reliable and cheap solution.

1.4.2 Shared display systems

This is the generic name for a new range of proprietary logging and control equipment which all of the large instrumentation and control manufacturers have developed in the late 1970s. They are based on the concept of the VDU-based plant control room. Conventional control panels and control desks which support dozens or even hundreds of indicators, chart recorders, 3-term controllers, switches, etc., are replaced by a compact control desk which supports one or more VDUs and little else.

The operator can monitor and control an entire plant by means of a VDU and keyboard. Many pages of several VDU formats present information in numerical and graphical form. Changes to controller setpoints, remote switching and even control system reconfiguration (e.g. cascade control, see section 6.9.1) can be implemented from his keyboard. Alarm conditions are highlighted and printer logs are produced.

Behind the VDU desk lurk the inevitable microcomputer system, instrumentation cubicles and 3-term controllers. This latter function is rarely incorporated into the VDU control-microcomputer system so that control-loop integrity is maintained in the event of display system breakdown.

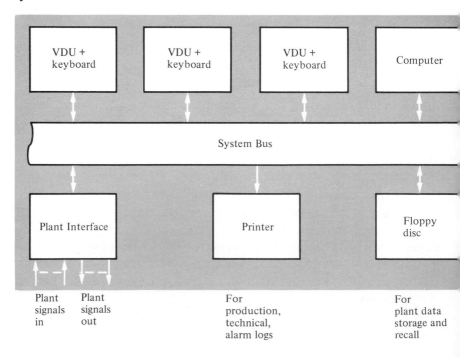

FIGURE 1.10 SHARED DISPLAY SYSTEM — EQUIPMENT CONFIGURATION

Figure 1.10 shows a typical equipment configuration. The computer, which is either a microcomputer or in some cases a more powerful and traditional minicomputer, communicates with its VDUs, printer, bulk storage (floppy disc normally) and the plant instrument and controller equipment through a data bus.

1.4.3 Factory robots

Microcomputer-based machine-positioning systems are becoming commonplace for automatic welding machines and lever/arm/grab position-control systems. They offer advantages over human control in terms of relative infallibility, lack of fatigue, speed and (when reprogrammed) flexibility. Typically several position-control systems are controlled to drive to different positions in a fixed sequence.

The concept of replacing a single position-control device (a "servomechanism" in its analogue form) by a microcomputer, which drives its transducers in digital form, is shown in Figures 1.11 (a) and 1.11 (b). The analogue system requires feedback to maximise position-control accuracy and overcome friction, striction and backlash. The microcomputer may operate with or without feedback; the stepper motor drives to a specific position and the shaft encoder records the precise position attained.

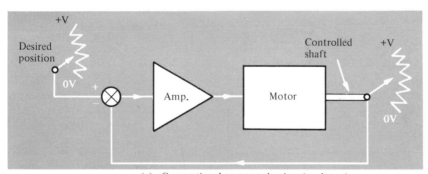

(a) Conventional servomechanism (analogue)

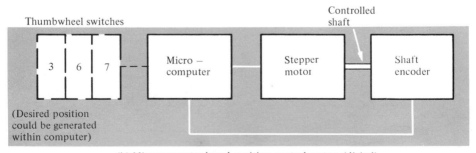

(b) Microcomputer-based position control system (digital)

FIGURE 1.11 ANALOGUE AND DIGITAL POSITION CONTROL SYSTEMS

1.4.4 Numerical control

Numerical Control is the technique of automatically controlling drilling and cutting machine tools to a pre-defined sequence of operations. Tailored minicomputers have been performing this type of control for many years. Microcomputers offer more cost-effective solutions.

Figure 1.12 shows the basic elements in a Numerical Control system. The pattern of cutting/drilling operations is prepared offline in magnetic tape or paper tape form. This tape is read into the computer which directly controls the machine tool to the pattern specified.

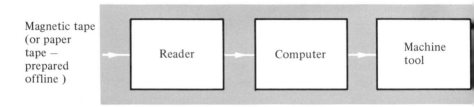

Magnetic tape (or paper tape — prepared offline)

FIGURE 1.12 NUMERICAL CONTROL

1.4.5 Programmable logic controller (PLC)

PLCs, which were not microcomputer based, were logic and sequence control systems which read several on/off (digital) signals from plant. The PLC could be programmed by a wire-patching system to produce a particular sequence, with time delays, of output signals to control plant operation. The latest PLCs, which are based on microcomputers, produce a much more flexible package. Figure 1.13 shows how a miniaturised VDU indicates an electrical analogy of the logic sequence which the system designer wishes to program into the device. The designer uses paper and pencil to prepare the logical control sequence on specially formatted preparation sheets. He then enters this sequence on the electrical circuit VDU format.

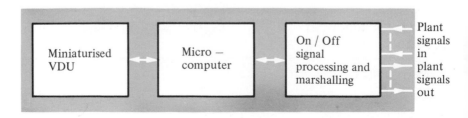

FIGURE 1.13 PROGRAMMABLE LOGIC CONTROLLER (PLC)

1.4.6 3-term controllers

Traditional pneumatic and electronic 3-term controllers for accurate control of process flow, temperature, pressure, level, etc., are now being replaced by microcomputer-based controllers.

Figure 1.14 shows in a simplified manner how the controller functions. The setpoint, which can be manually set or transmitted from a Shared Display System, is compared with the Measured Value, or plant reading. Corrective action is generated to drive the activator.

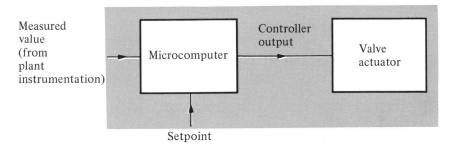

FIGURE 1.14 3-TERM CONTROLLER

A convenient method of displaying and altering the controller settings (e.g. proportional band, integral action time) is provided and these values can even be transmitted downline from a remote computer.

1.5 "HIDDEN" MICROCOMPUTERS

In many instances equipment is bought without the purchaser being aware that the intelligent heart of the device is in fact a microcomputer. Equipment which is bought to connect to or test a microcomputer is itself microcomputer based. Examples are as follows:

1.5.1 Teleprinters

Several quality teleprinters use a microcomputer for an automatic self-test print routine which is called when the device is switched on. The microcomputer also assists with serial data drive and character decoding.

1.5.2 Plotters

Hard copy graph plotters which are sometimes used in draughting and scientific applications also possess a microcomputer-based test plot routine.

1.5.3 Digital voltmeter (DVM)

The standard DVM is now being increasingly constructed around a microcomputer, which provides functions such as self-calibration, averaging of a number of measurements and automatic addition of an offset value.

1.6 TELECOMMUNICATIONS

As with process-control applications the telecommunications industry has not yet fully exploited the microprocessor. However, the British telephone system has committed itself to the introduction of "System X", which is the microcomputer (mainly the powerful 16-bit Intel 8086) and minicomputer-based telephone call switching and routing system. The first elements of this system—local exchange digital switching—will be introduced in 1983. The system will be extended to cover digital trunk exchanges by the mid-1980s.

Additionally the telephone-based information system Prestel (or "Viewdata"), which uses the domestic television receiver for display purposes, will become increasingly dependent on the microcomputer. Furthermore, Teletext, which is a similar system but uses conventional television transmission, is already applying microcomputers in its information display formatting. Ceefax is the name of the BBC system and Oracle that of the ITV system.

Even the newspaper industry has been involved in a confrontation over use of the microcomputer in its labour-saving type-setting application.

1.7 SINGLE-BOARD COMPUTERS

A large number of manufacturers produce cheap and compact single-board computers which are directed at the training and hobbyist market.

A typical board layout is shown in Figure 1.15. The manufacturer mounts the microprocessor prominently together with its memory and input/output chip so that the user can readily observe and test circuit operation. Programs can be entered using the keyboard and decimal display. Some boards have the facility to drive to a domestic television monitor to enable easier display of program instructions which are entered. Test switches and LEDs are typical accessories to enable the trainee to test programs in a simulated manner.

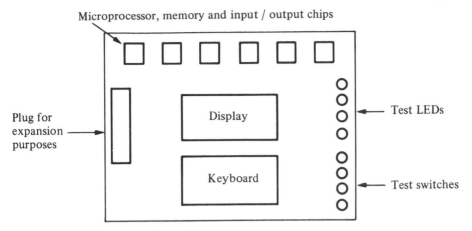

FIGURE 1.15 TYPICAL BOARD LAYOUT FOR MICROCOMPUTER TRAINING BOARD

1.8 MISCELLANEOUS APPLICATIONS

Other areas of application are:

1.8.1 Computer-aided design

The microcomputer's flexibility in terms of re-calculating a design in various forms is utilised in the computer-aided design application. Computer programs have been written to assist in the design of:

ARCHITECTURAL DRAWINGS—3-dimensional drawings can be rotated, re-dimensioned and re-positioned on a VDU.

MACHINED PIECES—an item for milling can be drawn on a VDU by the computer from a specification of dimensions.

ELECTRONIC CIRCUITS—can be designed, simulated and optimised.

CIRCUIT BOARD LAYOUT can be selected, altered and displayed in an iterative manner by computer program.

In all of these cases the final design can be copied from the VDU to a high-resolution plotter or to a video photocopier.

1.8.2 Computer-assisted learning

The learning machine is becoming increasingly used in schools and other teaching establishments. In these systems the pupil operates a simple keyboard to call a succession of information and question pages on the VDU. Impersonalised it may be, but the machine has many advantages in terms of quality of well-prepared information and an instruction rate which is controlled by the pupil.

1.8.3 Various military applications

The microcomputer is used in automatic tank gun-control systems which compensate for speed and direction of tank, wind velocity, etc., and in many other similar applications.

1.9 FUTURE APPLICATIONS

Whilst the list of existing applications, which are summarised above, is not exhaustive, similarly any predicted range of applications for the ubiquitous micro will be incomplete and speculative. However, a summary of future areas of application must include:

1.9.1 Home computer

There is little doubt that large numbers of householders will soon have access to their own microcomputer. These machines will be capable of performing household accounting, game playing, etc., and will have the communication features shown in Figure 1.16. The range of facilities which will be assessed via the telephone network will enable ordering of goods, seat reservations, transmission of documentary information (in place of letters) and many other features.

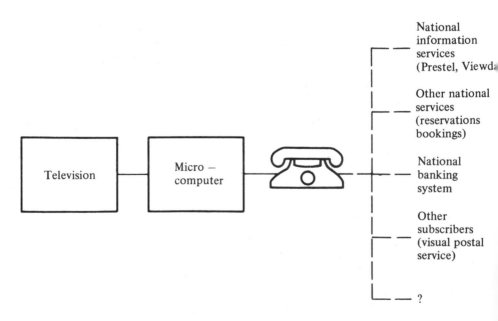

FIGURE 1.16 FUTURE HOME COMPUTER

1.9.2 Factory automation

Increasingly microcomputers will assist with process measurement and control. Automation of repetitive processes and more complex control requirements will escalate as more microcomputer solutions are developed for a multiplicity of engineering and production requirements. The day of the automatic factory will be approached.

1.9.3 Business applications

As the computing power in terms of computer program size, data file size, speed of processing and therefore computer throughput increases, the microcomputer will become indispensible for much larger-scale applications than apply at present. Additionally small organisations will increasingly turn to the use of cheap microcomputer systems for fast and convenient information filing and retrieval. Networks of microcomputers will become commonplace for information and facility sharing.

FURTHER READING

1. Shelley, J., *Microfuture,* Pitman, London, 1981.
2. Lund, R.J., *et al. Microprocessor Applications,* HMSO, London, 1980.
3. Swords-Isherwood, N. & Senker, P., *Microelectronics and the Engineering Industry,* Frances Pinter, London, 1980.
4. Rada, J., *The Impact of Microelectronics,* ILO, Geneva, 1981.

Chapter 2

Microcomputer Technology

2.1 NUMBER SYSTEMS

The normal decimal numbering system (sometimes called the DENARY system) uses a base of 10.

Thus Denary $382 = 3 \times 10^2 + 8 \times 10^1 + 2 \times 10^0$
$$= 300 + 80 + 2$$

Denary 382 can be written as 382_{10}

Computers use DIGITAL circuits to represent numbers, i.e. a transistor is switched ON or OFF, or a voltage is HIGH or LOW. Therefore there are two states which can be represented. The numbering system which computers use is called the BINARY system in which a binary digit (or "bit") can have one of two values: 0 or 1. Its base is 2.

Thus binary $101 = 1 \times 2^2 + 0 \times 2^1 + 1 \times 2^0$
$$= 4 + 0 + 1$$
$$= 5$$

Binary 101 can be written as 101_2

Binary numbers tend to be long. If binary digits are grouped into sets of four, the number is converted to a HEXADECIMAL base. This coding system enables binary numbers to become more manageable,

e.g. 1100 0110 1010
$$= C \ 6 \ A = C6A_{16}$$

This method of describing binary numbers is commonly used with microcomputers.

Thus the hexadecimal numbering system uses a base of 16,

e.g. Hexadecimal $C3 = 12 \times 16^1 + 3 \times 16^0 \ (C_{16} = 12_{10})$
$$= 192 + 3 = 195_{10}$$

Table 2.1 summarises these number systems.

TABLE 2.1 NUMBER SYSTEMS

Denary	Binary	Hexadecimal
0	0000	0
1	0001	1
2	0010	2
3	0011	3
4	0100	4
5	0101	5
6	0110	6
7	0111	7
8	1000	8
9	1001	9
10	1010	A
11	1011	B
12	1100	C
13	1101	D
14	1110	E
15	1111	F

Thus, denary (decimal) 11 = hexadecimal 8
and, denary (decimal) 16 = hexadecimal 10.

An alternative numbering system was traditionally used with many previous computers but is rarely used with microcomputers. This is the OCTAL system, in which binary digits are grouped into sets of 3.

$$\text{e.g. } 101 \quad 011 \quad 111$$
$$= \quad 5 \quad \ \ 3 \quad \ \ 7 \quad = 537_8$$

Exercise 2.1

Convert $1011\ 0011_2$ to hexadecimal.

Answer: 1011 0011
$$= \quad B \quad \ \ 3 \quad = B3_{16}$$

Exercise 2.2

Convert $D4_{16}$ to binary.

Answer: 1101   0100 = 11010100_2

Exercise 2.3

Convert $A7_{16}$ to denary (decimal).

Answer: A7
$$= 10 \times 16^1 + 7 \times 16^0$$
$$= 160 + 7 = 167_{10}$$

Note that microcomputers commonly group bits into 8-bit group called BYTES. Thus, 1 byte comprises two hexadecimal codes.

2.2 LOGICAL FUNCTIONS

Whilst the microcomputer can perform the normal arithmetical operations (addition, subtraction, multiplication and division) on binary numbers, it can also perform the following LOGICAL operations:

2.2.1 OR operation

If either one of two binary digits (bits) is 1, then the OR operation produces a 1. Otherwise 0 is produced.

Using the Boolean symbol + for OR:

$$0+0=0$$
$$0+1=1$$
$$1+0=1$$
$$1+1=1$$

This can be summarised in the TRUTH TABLE 2.2:

TABLE 2.2 TRUTH TABLE FOR OR GATE

A	B	A+B
0	0	0
0	1	1
1	0	1
1	1	1

2.2.2 AND operation

If both of two binary digits (bits) are 1, then the AND operation produces a 1. Otherwise 0 if produced.

Using the Boolean symbol $\odot$ (dot) for AND:

$$0.0=0$$
$$0.1=0$$
$$1.0=0$$
$$1.1=1$$

This can be summarised in the Truth Table 2.3:

TABLE 2.3 TRUTH TABLE FOR AND GATE

A	B	A.B
0	0	0
0	1	0
1	0	0
1	1	1

2.2.3 EXCLUSIVE OR operation

If two binary digits (bits) are different, the EXCLUSIVE OR operation produces a 1. Otherwise 0 is produced.

Using the Boolean symbol $\oplus$ for EXCLUSIVE OR:

$$0 \oplus 0 = 0$$
$$0 \oplus 1 = 1$$
$$1 \oplus 0 = 1$$
$$1 \oplus 1 = 0$$

This can be summarised in Truth Table 2.4:

TABLE 2.4 TRUTH TABLE FOR EXCLUSIVE OR GATE

A	B	$A \oplus B$
0	0	0
0	1	1
1	0	1
1	1	0

2.2.4 NOT operation

This operation simply complements a binary digit. A bar is placed over a digit to represent NOT,

$$\text{i.e. } \overline{A} = \text{NOT A}$$
$$\overline{1} = 0$$
$$\overline{0} = 1$$

2.3 INTEGRATED CIRCUITS

Integrated circuits have evolved from the original discrete component electronic circuits. The term "integrated" implies that several components (transistors, resistors, etc.) are combined into a single device.

Until fairly recently most integrated circuits were constructed using BI POLAR devices (i.e. both P- and N-type semiconductor material is used) using the PLANAR EPITAXIAL fabrication technique. In this technique areas of P and N type are formed in a base slab of silicon by a masking, photo-resist and vapour deposition process. Similar fabrication techniques are used with the most recent devices called UNIPOLAR devices (i.e. current is conveyed by one type of carrier only). The type of transistor used with these devices is the field effect transistor (FET) and integrated circuits using these devices are called

MPC–C

MOS (metal oxide silicon) circuits. A variation of the basic MOS circuit is the complementary circuit called CMOS. Both MOS and CMOS are particularly attractive for microcomputer circuits because of their small area of fabrication and low power consumption. However, the more conventional bipolar circuits still represent the most common devices for generalised digital and microcomputer application. They are significantly faster than unipolar devices. Additionally CMOS circuits are easily damaged by static voltages caused by careless handling.

The first types of logic circuits which were made in integrated circuit form were RTL (resistor transistor logic) and DTL (diode transistor logic). These have been largely replaced by TTL (transistor transistor logic) which is bipolar and MOS/CMOS which are unipolar.

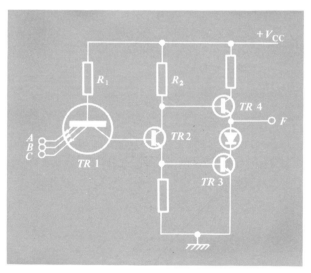

FIGURE 2.1 TTL NAND GATE

Figure 2.1 shows a TTL NAND (NOT AND) gate. When all the inputs are at logic 1 (+5 V) the output is at logic 0 (0 V); otherwise the output is at logic 1.

Figure 2.2 shows a CMOS NOR (NOT OR) gate. When both inputs are at logic 0 the output is at logic 1; otherwise the output is at logic 1.

The most common package for integrated circuits is the dual-in-line (DIL) package, as shown in Figure 2.3. The number of connection pins varies from 4 to 40. Most microprocessors require the largest 40-pin package. There is no doubt that when more powerful micro-

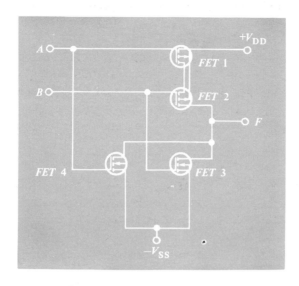

FIGURE 2.2 CMOS NOR GATE

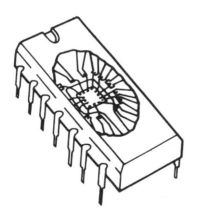

FIGURE 2.3 DIL PACKAGE

processors (perhaps 32-bit machines) are developed, larger DILs, perhaps up to 100-pin units, will be used.

A fairly simple example of a DIL integrated circuit is the SN 7400, which is a TTL device consisting of four NAND gates, as shown in Figure 2.4. An enormous range of circuits including gates, multivibrators, counters, computer memories and microprocessors, is manufactured in this integrated circuit form. Even analogue circuits,

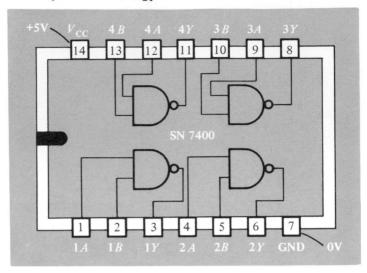

FIGURE 2.4 SN 7400 4-NAND GATES

e.g. operational amplifiers, are produced in integrated circuits.
Note the following definitions:

SMALL-SCALE INTEGRATION   up to 10 devices/chip
MEDIUM-SCALE INTEGRATION   up to 100 devices/chip
LARGE-SCALE INTEGRATION   up to a few thousand
                                            devices/chip
VERY LARGE-SCALE INTEGRATION   tens of thousands of devices/chip

Microprocessors fall into this last category.

2.4. MAIN ELEMENTS IN A MICROCOMPUTER

The main elements in a microcomputer are shown in Figure 2.5.

The microprocessor is commonly called the CPU (central processor unit). It is normally mounted on a single chip. The microprocessor does not normally possess any on-chip memory. One or more memory chips stores the computer program and data. Communication in and out of the microcomputer to operator's VDU, printer, indicating lamps, etc., is via the Input/Output. Again this may consist of one or more chips.

The microprocessor (CPU) obeys a "program" which is a series of "instructions". An instruction directs the microprocessor to perform a specific function, e.g. add two numbers, send some data out through the Input/Output unit, etc.

There are three signal "buses" as follows:

ADDRESS BUS which carries a memory address (of a program instruction or an item of data) or an input/output address (to transfer data in or out of the microprocessor).

DATA BUS which carries a program instruction or data item which is addressed by the address bus.

CONTROL BUS which performs timing and sequence control of the above actions.

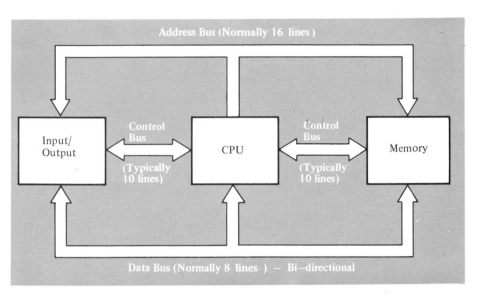

FIGURE 2.5 BLOCK DIAGRAM OF MICROCOMPUTER

2.5 THE CPU

The CPU, or microprocessor, is the intelligent heart of the microcomputer. It contains several registers which are used to provide temporary storage of program instructions and data items. One special register is called the ACCUMULATOR and this contains the result of all arithmetic and logic operations.

A generalised block diagram, which is typical of most microprocessors, is shown in Figure 2.6.

Notice the Address and Data Buses leaving the microprocessor and connecting to the Memory and Input/Output. The Control Bus is not shown to avoid over-complexity.

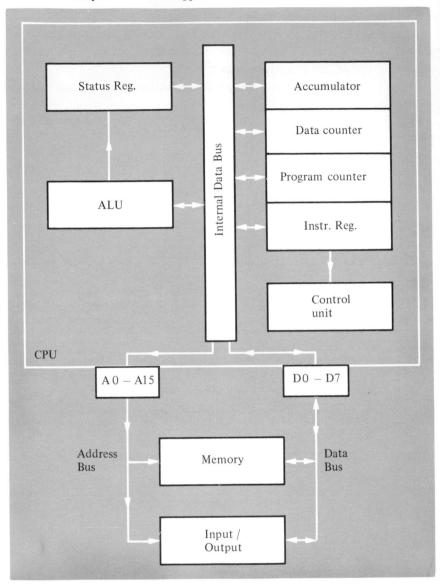

FIGURE 2.6 BLOCK DIAGRAM OF CPU

There are four main registers:

ACCUMULATOR—this holds data that has been fetched from memory and also holds the result of any arithmetical or logical operations.

DATA COUNTER—this holds the memory address which data is being written to or read from.

PROGRAM COUNTER—this holds the address of the memory word
from which the next instruction code will be fetched.

INSTRUCTION REGISTER—this holds the instruction which the CPU is
currently obeying.

The diagram in Figure 2.6 applies to an 8-bit microprocessor, which
is still by far the most common type. In these devices the Accumulator
and Instruction Register are 8 bits in length and the other two registers
(Data Counter and Program Counter) are 16 bits. In these latter
cases the 16 bits allow up to 64,000 memory locations to be specified
($2^{16} = 64,000$ or 64 K).

The CONTROL UNIT is a complex piece of circuitry which decodes the
current instruction which is held in the Instruction register. It sends
out control signals around the CPU to allow data flow between the
registers, through the ALU and also beyond the CPU (to Memory
and Input/Output). The combination and timing of these control signals is different for each instruction type.

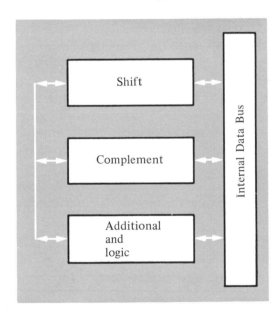

FIGURE 2.7 THE ALU

The ALU, or Arithmetic and Logic Unit, performs the arithmetical, logical and some additional functions as shown in Figure 2.7.
Essentially it is the intelligent kernel of the CPU. Its main operations
are:

BINARY ADDITION. Using binary addition the other three arithmetic
processes can be accomplished, viz. subtraction (the CPU forms

a negated form of the number, called two's complement, and then performs addition), multiplication (the CPU performs this function by a shifting and adding process) and division (successive shifting and subtracting).

LOGICAL OPERATIONS. These are AND, OR and EXCLUSIVE OR. An additional function is COMPARE.

COMPLEMENT. This function performs bit inversion on a data word.

SHIFT. This shifts a data word one bit to the right or left and also performs multi-bit shift.

One final component of the CPU which requires description is the STATUS REGISTER. This is not really a register at all, but rather is a collection of memory elements which are status flags. These flags are set as a result of ALU operations. They comprise:

CARRY STATUS FLAG—set when arithmetic operations in the ALU cause a carry bit to be generated.

ZERO STATUS FLAG—this is set to indicate that a data manipulation operation generated a zero result.

SIGN STATUS FLAG—this is set to the sign of the data value last processed by the ALU (note that if a binary number is positive the most significant bit is the sign bit and is set to 0; if the number is negative the sign bit is set to 1).

PARITY STATUS FLAG—this is set each time a data transfer operation detects that a data byte has the wrong parity (e.g. the 8th bit of byte code for keyboard characters is commonly added to form even parity, so that adding all the 1s in the code produces an even number.

OVERFLOW STATUS FLAG—this is set when the result of an ALU operation is larger than the largest number which can be handled by the machine.

Most instructions in a program ignore these Status Flags but it is useful occasionally to check the results of an arithmetic or logic operation to decide which course of action the computer program should take.

The general principle of operation of the CPU is that it takes a series of instructions in turn from Memory, reads them into its instruction Register and uses the Control Unit and ALU to implement these instructions.

2.6 THE FETCH/EXECUTE CYCLE

When the CPU implements each instruction, two clearly defined actions occur:

FETCH—the instruction is fetched from memory to the CPU.

EXECUTE—the instruction is executed within the CPU. This involves examining the instruction (in the Control Unit), fetching more data if required and finally implementing the actions which the instruction code requires.

The Fetch action is identical for every instruction and its operation is shown in Figure 2.8. The memory address held in the Program

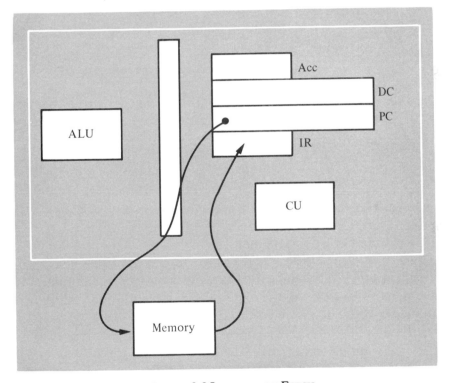

FIGURE 2.8 INSTRUCTION FETCH

Counter is sent via the Address Bus to Memory. The Instruction Code byte is then read in on the Data Bus to the Instruction Register.

Let us assume that the Instruction Code is demanding that the CPU fetches the contents of the data word which is addressed by the Data Counter and stores it in the Accumulator. Therefore the action of the

Execute half of the process is to decode the instruction in the Control Unit and to bring in the data word to the CPU as shown in Figure 2.9.

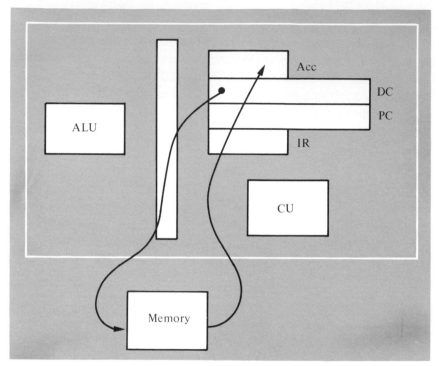

FIGURE 2.9 INSTRUCTION EXECUTE — MOVE THE CONTENTS OF THE MEMORY LOCATION HELD IN DATA COUNTER TO ACCUMULATOR

The instruction is now complete.

Consider now a more complex instruction: "Add from memory to Accumulator". Additionally the Data Counter does not already hold the memory address of the data word. Instead, that address is specified in the instruction as shown in Figure 2.10.

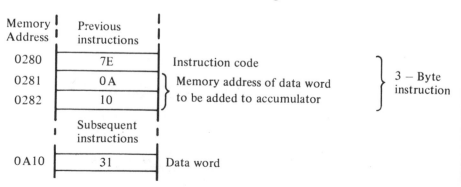

FIGURE 2.10 MEMORY LAYOUT OF INSTRUCTION "ADD FROM MEMORY"

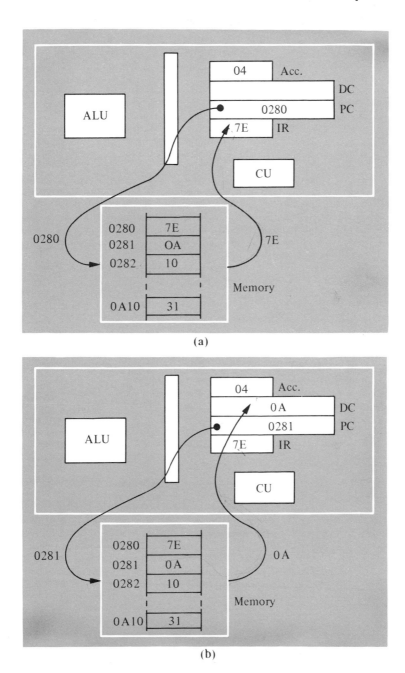

(a)

(b)

FIGURE 2.11(a) "ADD FROM MEMORY" — INSTRUCTION (OPERATOR) FETCH
FIGURE 2.11(b) "ADD FROM MEMORY" — FETCH HIGH ORDER HALF OF
DATA ADDRESS

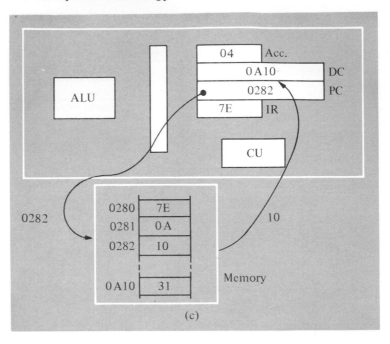

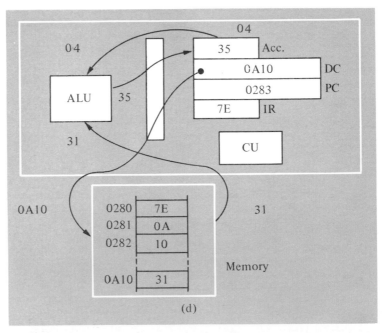

FIGURE 2.11(c) "ADD FROM MEMORY" — FETCH LOW ORDER HALF OF
DATA ADDRESS

FIGURE 2.11(d) "ADD FROM MEMORY" — FETCH DATA AND
ADD TO ACCUMULATOR

Notice that three bytes or memory words are required to hold this instruction. Often the first byte is termed the instruction OPERATOR, and the second two bytes are termed the instruction OPERAND. The Operand can refer to a memory address, as in this case, or even a data value directly.

Notice also that the data word is held well separated in Memory from the program—address 0A10 for data word compared with 0281 for program. A good programmer always clearly segregates his program and data areas.

If we assume that the Accumulator previously held the number 4, the operation of this instruction is shown in Figure 2.11 (a) to 2.11 (d).

The instruction (operator part) is first fetched in the usual manner from Memory address 0280 as shown in Figure 2.11 (a). Then the first (most significant) part of the data address is read in from 0281 and placed in the top half of the Data Counter, as shown in Figure 2.11 (b). The second half of this address is read in in a similar manner, as shown in Figure 2.11 (c). Finally the addition operation is performed through the ALU is the last (rather hectic!) step in the procedure, as shown in Figure 2.11 (d) and summarised as follows:

(a) the Memory address 0A10 is sent to Memory;
(b) the data value 31 is read into the ALU;
(c) simultaneously with (b) the Accumulator contents 04 are also conveyed to the ALU;
(d) the result 35 of the addition in the ALU is conveyed back to the Accumulator.

Notice that the Program Counter has been automatically incremented at each stage of this procedure and now stands at 0283, ready for the next instruction.

All of these actions are "clocked", i.e. triggered by the system clock. This is normally crystal controlled and may run at a frequency of 2 MHz, 4 MHz or even faster. Commonly two or more "ticks" of this clock occur for each of the steps described above. A typical execution time for the instructions described above is 3 to 10 microseconds.

2.7 ROM MEMORY

There are two types of semiconductor memory, ROM (read only memory) and RAM (random access memory). These names represent a complete misnomer since ROM is also random access memory. In fact these names represent a classical misrepresentation in the history of electronics, but we are stuck with them. Better definitions are:

ROM—information can only be read from ROM devices,
RAM—information can be read from *and* written to RAM devices.
RAM devices are described in the next section.
ROM memory chips are available in a variety of sizes, e.g. 1024 memory locations, each location is 1 byte. This is often written 1024 × 8. 64K byte ROMs are not now uncommon.

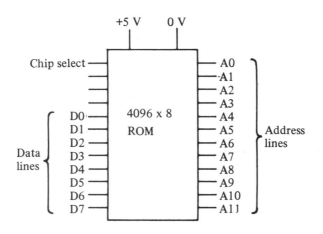

FIGURE 2.12 ROM CHIP

Figure 2.12 shows the pin connections to a 4096 × 8 ROM chip. Apart from the d.c. supply wires there are three groups of connections:

(a) DATA LINES (D0–D7)—data is read from ROM to the CPU on this highway.
(b) ADDRESS LINES (A0–A11)—the memory byte which is selected is addressed with a unique address on these 12 lines.
Notice $2^{12} = 4096$, which is the storage capacity of the chip.
(c) CHIP SELECT—the chip will only present its data on the Data Lines if this control signal is set to logical 1 (+5 V). The Chip Select is produced as a result of external decoding on the more significant address lines A12–A15. Sometimes two Chip Select (CS) signals are connected to ROM chips. In these cases CS1 must be low and CS2 must be high to activate the chip.

There are several different types of ROM called ROM, PROM, EPROM and EAROM as follows:

2.7.1 ROM

This is factory programmed and program instructions and data once written cannot be altered. It is generally used for mass-produced and fixed memory applications and is the cheapest semiconductor memory device.

2.7.2 PROM

Programmable ROM (PROM) is manufactured in a "blank" form and is programmed by the customer. Once programmed by a "fusible-link" process in a PROM programmer it cannot subsequently be re-programmed.

2.7.3 EPROM

Erasable Programmable ROM is used for development applications and in situations in which it is required to re-program the ROM. EPROM can be cleared (all storage bits set to 1) by exposing the chip to ultra-violet (UV) light for at least 10 minutes. The light enters the chip through a glass window in the package.

2.7.4 EAROM

Electrically Alterable ROM is used where it is required to erase small parts, e.g. 1 word, of ROM. It is rarely used.

Note that a program stored on ROM is often called "FIRMWARE".

2.8 RAM MEMORY

RAM is more complex and expensive than ROM because data can be written to RAM as well as read from it. Because a RAM chip contains more circuitry than ROM it is available in much smaller memory capacities. For this reason RAM chips commonly hold 1, 2 or 4 bits. Therefore if byte storage is required two or more chips have to be placed in parallel on a data bus as shown in Figure 2.13.

Notice that the left-hand RAM stores the first 4 data bits using D0–D3 and the right-hand RAM stores the second 4 bits using D4–D7. Clearly the Data Lines are bi-directional to handle read and write operations.

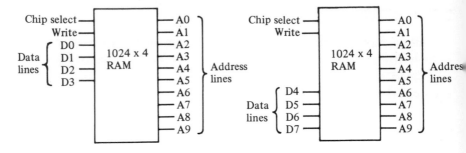

FIGURE 2.13 RAM STORAGE FOR 1024 BYTES

An additional control signal is required for RAM to distinguish between read and write operations. This is the WRITE signal (write when set, read when not set). The CHIP SELECT signal effectively "switches on" the chip for both read and write operations.

The 10 Address Lines give an addressing range of 1024. Occasionally a block address is burnt into the chip, i.e. additional more significant address lines are taken to the chip such that the chip only responds when these lines are set in a particular combination.

2.9 INPUT/OUTPUT

Each microprocessor manufacturer supports his master chip with input/output chips. These are as diverse and as variable in operation as the microprocessors themselves. However, a generalised design is shown in Figure 2.14.

The Address and Data Buses connect to such a chip just as for Memory. Different Control Lines are normally used, however. READ and WRITE distinguish between input and output data transfers. INPUT/OUTPUT SELECTED performs a Chip Select function and distinguishes between Memory and Input/Output. CLOCK is used to trigger data transfers at a timing rate which is determined by the CPU.

The signal lines which connect to external devices are shown on the left-hand side of Figure 2.14; 16 is a typical number of lines, and these lines are often grouped into sets of 8 and called "ports". In this case the two ports could be used to drive input/output devices such as LED indicators, switches, keyboard plus display, floppy-disc drive, etc. In some microcomputers input/output is "memory mapped", i.e. input/output uses the same set of instructions and the same set of control signals as memory devices. Clearly memory and input/output chips must not have identical addresses in this situation, e.g. memory may

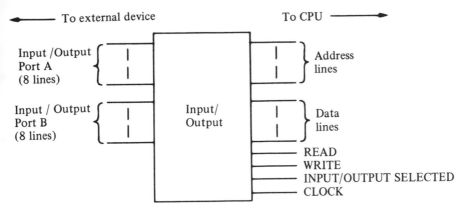

FIGURE 2.14 PARALLEL INPUT/OUTPUT CHIP

extend from hexadecimal 000 to 2FF and input/output may extend from 300 to 3FF.

A different type of input/output device is one which drives data to or from external devices in a serial form. Such devices are called UART (Universal Asynchronous Receiver Transmitter) and USART (a synchronous version of a UART) chips. The principle of a UART, which is the more common device, is shown in Figure 2.15. For transmission, i.e. output, of data a byte is sent from the CPU to the UART on the Data Bus. The UART performs a parallel/serial conversion procedure using a shift register and the data is pulsed to the external device. Serial input/output is particularly beneficial over long distances because the number of cable cores is reduced (just two in each direction). Typical external devices are a printer or a data link to another microcomputer.

Some parallel input/output chips have additional features such as the ability to handle interrupts (these will be described later) to the CPU and to perform interval timing.

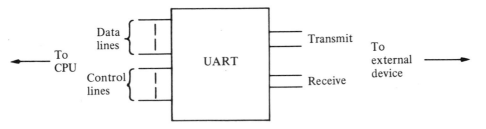

FIGURE 2.15 UART FOR SERIAL INPUT/OUTPUT

2.10 THE BUS SYSTEM

The microprocessor has three buses: Address, Data and Control.

2.10.1 Address bus

The Address Bus selects the particular memory or Input/Output device, and the precise location within that device, which is to communicate with the Data Bus. Some block decoding system is necessary to distinguish between one Memory chip and another and one Input/Output chip and another.

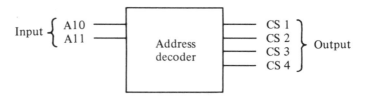

FIGURE 2.16 ADDRESS DECODER

Such a decoding circuit is shown in Figure 2.16. This is a "four-from-two" decoder in which only one of the output CS lines is set for each combination of the input 2-bit address code according to the Truth Table 2.5:

TABLE 2.5 TRUTH TABLE FOR ADDRESS DECODER

A11	A10	CS1	CS2	CS3	CS4
0	0	1	0	0	0
0	1	0	1	0	0
1	0	0	0	1	0
1	1	0	0	0	1

Figure 2.17 shows how these individual Chip Select signals are used to activate one of three ROM chips. The particular byte or location within the ROM selected is determined by the settings of A0–A9 (10 bits, $2^{10} = 1024$ addresses). Notice that CS4 is not used; this particular configuration has a total of only 3K ROM.

Notice also that in this practical circuit there are two Enable (or Chip Select) signals to the Address Decoder chip itself. Without these signals being set correctly the Decoder will place logical 0 on CS1 to CS4 and no ROM will be activated. $\overline{EN}$ is only set when the control signal READ is set by the CPU. EN is only set when the more significant address lines A12–A15 are set to 0. Thus these more significant address lines could feed an additional Address Decoder circuit to provide block addressing (using Chip Select signals) to other ROM or RAM devices. Table 2.6 lists the address combinations for this particular configuration.

TABLE 2.6 ADDRESSING SYSTEM FOR THREE 1024 × 8 ROM SYSTEM

	Other device select				ROM select		Location within ROM											Hex	Decimal
Address Bit:	15	14	13	12	11	10	9	8	7	6	5	4	3	2	1	0		Hex	Decimal
ROM 1	0	0	0	0	0	0	0	0	0	0	0	0	0	0	0	0	0000	0000
	0	0	0	0	0	0	0	0	0	0	0	0	0	0	0	1	0001	0001
	0	0	0	0	0	0	0	0	0	0	0	0	0	0	1	0	0002	0002
	0	0	0	0	0	0	1	1	1	1	1	1	1	1	1	1	03FF	1023
ROM 2	0	0	0	0	0	1	0	0	0	0	0	0	0	0	0	0	0400	1024
	0	0	0	0	0	1	0	0	0	0	0	0	0	0	0	1	0401	1025
	0	0	0	0	0	1	0	0	0	0	0	0	0	0	1	0	0402	1026
	0	0	0	0	0	1	1	1	1	1	1	1	1	1	1	1	07FF	2047
ROM 3	0	0	0	0	1	0	0	0	0	0	0	0	0	0	0	0	0800	2048
	0	0	0	0	1	0	0	0	0	0	0	0	0	0	0	1	0801	2049
	0	0	0	0	1	0	0	0	0	0	0	0	0	0	1	0	0802	2050
	0	0	0	0	1	0	1	1	1	1	1	1	1	1	1	1	0BFF	3071
Not used	0	0	0	0	1	1	0	0	0	0	0	0	0	0	0	0	0C00	3072
	0	0	0	0	1	1	1	1	1	1	1	1	1	1	1	1	0FFF	4095
Other devices	0	0	0	1	0	0	0	0	0	0	0	0	0	0	0	0	1000	4096

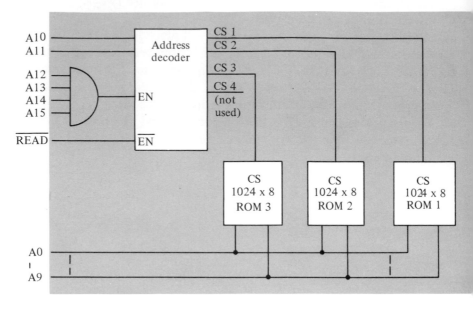

FIGURE 2.17 ADDRESS DECODING FOR THREE 1024 × 8 ROM

2.10.2 Data bus

The problem with any data bus system is that more than one device may be trying to write data onto it or read data from it at the same time. This is solved in the microcomputer using a "Tri-state" Data Bus. The three states of the data lines are:

LOGICAL 0, i.e. the bit is not set,

LOGICAL 1, i.e. the bit is set,

FLOATING, i.e. no device has been selected and all of the data lines float high.

Only one device can be selected at a time using the address decoding and Chip Select system described above. Each device which can be selected (ROM, RAM, Input/Output and even the CPU itself for data write operation) has a three-state driver at its output or input. Figure 2.18 shows the principle of operation of a Memory or Input/Output device drive onto the Data Bus. If no device is using the Data Bus its lines are floating. If this particular device is activated, then its Chip Select will gate its 8 data output signals onto the Data Bus. The Data Bus lines will be set to Logical 0 and 1 as appropriate.

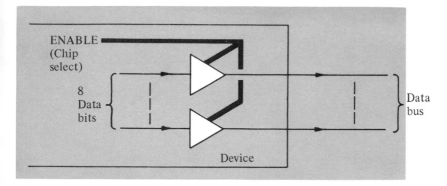

FIGURE 2.18 OUTPUT DRIVERS FOR A TRI-STATE DEVICE

2.10.3 Control bus

READ, WRITE, INPUT/OUTPUT SELECTED (not necessary if Input/Output is memory mapped) and CLOCK (for Input/Output timing) are the only control signals which have been encountered so far. There are a few more control lines which handle interrupts and DMA operations which will be described in the following sections titled DMA and Interrupts.

2.11 DMA (DIRECT MEMORY ACCESS)

When microcomputers wish to pass data from Input/Output to Memory, or vice versa, that data is normally passed through the CPU under control of a program which the CPU runs. Occasionally microcomputers use a facility whereby data is transferred between Input/Output and Memory directly, as shown in Figure 2.19. The DMA Controller generates a HOLD signal which causes the CPU to stop all of its operations after the current instruction is completed. The CPU responds with a HOLDA (Hold Acknowledge) signal. The DMA Controller then causes data to be transferred directly between Input/Output and Memory using the Address and Data Buses.

There are three methods of timing DMA transfers:

(a) HOLD CPU every instruction (or few instructions) when 1 data word is transferred.

(b) HOLD CPU until a complete block data transfer is complete.

(c) Do not delay CPU but transfer data words in "dead time" on Address and Data Buses, i.e. when Address and Data Buses are not being used during normal operation.

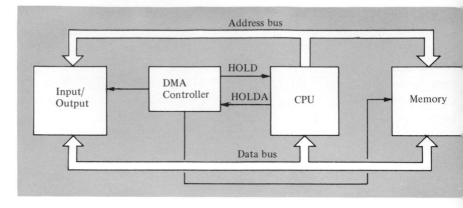

FIGURE 2.19 DMA OPERATION

DMA produces very rapid data transfer and is often used for communicating with peripheral devices such as hard disc or floppy disc. In these cases data transfer is initiated when the data starting position on the rotating disc has reached the position of the reading head. DMA transfers continue until the required number of data words is transferred.

2.12 SOFTWARE CONCEPTS

Normally microprocessors possess a small number of work registers which are additional to those mentioned so far. These enable data to be stored temporarily without the slower application of RAM and they make the job of programming the computer easier.

Most programs contain straightforward lists of instructions which are obeyed in sequence. Frequently, however, the sequence will be broken by one of the following variations.

2.12.1 Conditional jumps

Data is checked using the Status Flags described earlier and depending on the result program control may jump to a different section of program. Sometimes an unconditional jump is executed to another part of the program.

2.12.2 Program loops

A program loop is a set of instructions which is repeated more than once with each pass of the loop occurring in a consecutive manner. Thus if program control loops through a section, which processes just one item at a time, a list of items can be processed.

2.12.3 Subroutines

Sometimes it is beneficial to segregate a commonly used set of instructions so that several programs, or several parts of the same program, can call it. This program section is termed a SUBROUTINE. It saves memory space because the set of instructions does not have to be repeated in each program.

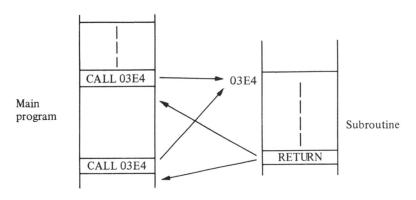

FIGURE 2.20 SUBROUTINE CALLING

Figure 2.20 demonstrates the principle. When the CALL instruction is obeyed the Subroutine is entered. The Subroutine terminates with a RETURN instruction which sends program control back to the main program (in fact to the instruction which followed the Subroutine call). The method by which the CPU remembers the location in the main program where program control should return is described in section 2.12.5 below.

2.12.4 Interrupts

Sometimes the microprocessor must react to events that are infrequent, unpredictable or require immediate action. In such cases the current program can be interrupted and a special interrupt subroutine entered. A return instruction at the end of the subroutine causes the program flow to return to the interrupted program.

The mechanism of an interrupted subroutine is very similar to that of an ordinary subroutine except that it is triggered by a hardware action (an interrupt signal wire to the CPU going high) and not a software CALL instruction.

The method which the CPU uses to select which memory address is the start of the interrupt subroutine for a particular interrupt line is by

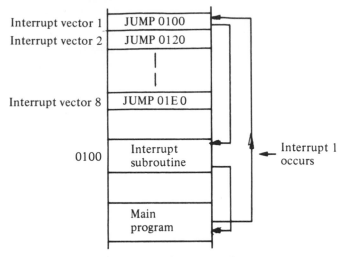

FIGURE 2.21 THE USE OF INTERRUPT VECTORS

the application of INTERRUPT VECTORS. Figure 2.21 shows how the CPU reserves some memory locations for instructions which cause program jumps to the various interrupt subroutines. When a particular interrupt occurs the CPU completes the current instruction which is being obeyed in the main program, extracts the appropriate interrupt vector from its reserved memory location and jumps to that interrupt subroutine. When this subroutine is completed operation of the main program is resumed.

It is possible to interrupt an interrupt subroutine. This gives rise to a NESTED INTERRUPT system. It is often useful to prevent some interrupts from occurring, e.g. if no interrupt subroutines exist for those interrupt signal lines, or if a high-priority interrupt subroutine must not be interrupted itself. Therefore a priority and masking system is designed into the CPU as shown in Figure 2.22. The interrupt Mask

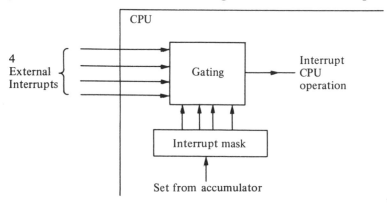

FIGURE 2.22 INTERRUPT MASKING

can be set by a program instruction and can be used to prevent interrupts below a certain priority occurring. Typically, microprocessors have a capacity of from 4 to 8 interrupt lines.

2.12.5 Stack

The use of a Stack is the normal method by which microprocessors store return addresses when subroutines (including interrupt subroutines) are executed. A Stack is simply a series of memory locations. Normally only the first of these locations is used when a subroutine is called, but if nested subroutine calls occur each return address is stored in sequential locations in the Stack. The microprocessor requires an additional register called the STACK POINTER to indicate the memory location of the last return address stored on the Stack. Program control returns to that address when the next RETURN instruction is implemented.

The use of the Stack is automatic as far as the Programmer is concerned. He simply uses CALL and RETURN instructions when using subroutines and leaves the CPU and Stack Pointer to handle the return addressing.

Figure 2.23 shows the principle of operation of a Stack. When the CALL instruction is obeyed and the Subroutine is entered, the return

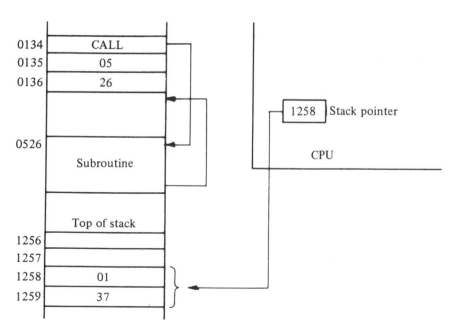

FIGURE 2.23 USE OF THE STACK AND STACK POINTER

address (0137) is stored on the Stack and the Stack Pointer is incremented to 1258. When the RETURN instruction is implemented the return address is taken from the Stack and placed in the Program Counter and program control resumes at that point in the main program. The Stack Pointer is decremented to 1256.

Occasionally the Stack is used manually, e.g. data rather than a return address can be stored. The PUSH (store on Stack) and POP (retrieve data from Stack) instructions are used.

2.12.6 Addressing modes

When program instructions refer to memory locations there are several possible addressing modes.

DIRECT ADDRESSING—the memory address specified contains the data required.

INDIRECT ADDRESSING—the memory address specified contains the address of the data required.

REGISTER, or IMPLIED, ADDRESSING—the memory address that holds the data required is stored in the Data Counter Register (one of the Work Registers).

IMMEDIATE ADDRESSING—the number presented in the Operand part of the instruction is not an address at all but is the data value required.

RELATIVE ADDRESSING—often used with conditional jump instructions; the Operand contains the step forwards or backwards in memory locations from the current address.

Not all of these addressing modes are available with all microprocessors. Additionally some microprocessors exhibit their own addressing options. One such feature is AUTO INCREMENT or AUTO DECREMENT. In this option the address referenced is incremented/decremented automatically when the instruction is obeyed. This saves the programmer having to add separate increment or decrement instructions if he requires the address to change.

A particularly powerful addressing option is INDEXED ADDRESSING, although only a few microprocessors possess it. It is similar to Direct Addressing except that the address specified is modified by the contents of one of the Work Registers. This is illustrated conceptually in Figure 2.24. Assume that the instruction held at 2005 is demanding "Move to the Accumulator the contents of 3005 modified/indexed by Work Register N". The Work Register contents, say 0002, are added to the address 3005 to produce 3007. Thus the contents of 3007 are actually conveyed to the Accumulator. This feature is particularly useful when data lists are being handled in program loops.

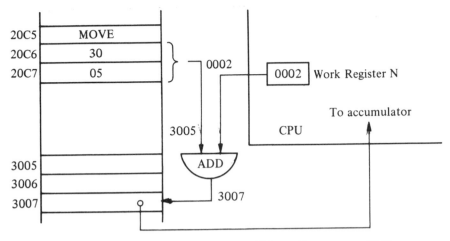

FIGURE 2.24 INDEXED ADDRESSING — "MOVE CONTENTS OF 3005
(INDEXED BY WORK REGISTER N) TO ACCUMULATOR

2.13 TYPICAL INSTRUCTION SET

Microprocessors typically have between 50 and 100 different instructions. Notice that for 8-bit microprocessors the maximum number of bit combinations is 256.

One of many ways of dividing up on Instruction Set is: Data Transfer Group, Arithmetic and Logic Group, Test and Branch Group, Miscellaneous. These are now described.

2.13.1 Data transfer group

MOVE instructions transfer data (or addresses) from one register to another.

LOAD instructions transfer data/addresses from a memory location to the CPU (Accumulator).

STORE instructions transfer data/addresses from the CPU (Accumulator) to memory.

INPUT/OUTPUT instructions transfer data between CPU (Accumulator) and external devices.

2.13.2 Arithmetic and logic group

ADD, SUBTRACT, MULTIPLY and DIVIDE instructions perform arithmetic operations and leave the result in the Accumulator.

LOGICAL (i.e. AND, OR, EXOR) instructions perform the logical operations and leave the result in the Accumulator.

INCREMENT/DECREMENT instructions add/subtract 1 (sometimes also 2) to register contents.

SHIFT instructions shift the bit pattern held in the Accumulator 1 or more bit positions to the left or right—these operations are useful when bit patterns need to be examined or masked in any way; they can also be used to multiply and divide by 2 (or multiples of 2).

2.13.3 Test and jump group

It is sensible to group the Compare and Conditional Jump instructions together because the two types are commonly applied together.

COMPARE instructions compare a data item, or the contents of a memory location or register, with the Accumulator. The Status Flags indicate the result of the comparison.

JUMP instructions examine one of the Status Flags and cause the program flow to jump to the specified location if that flag is set. One jump instruction will be unconditional.

CALL or BRANCH instructions are similar to an unconditional jump instruction, but they are used for entering subroutines such that the return address is stored on the Stack. The corresponding RETURN instruction causes re-entry to the main program.

2.13.4 Miscellaneous group

PUSH/POP instructions are for manual use of the Stack.

LOAD INTERRUPT MASK is used for preventing unwanted interrupts. Other interrupt control instructions are sometimes used, e.g. ENABLE INTERRUPTS, DISABLE INTERRUPTS.

One or two specialised additional instructions are sometimes added by microprocessor designers, e.g. HALT, RESTART.

Notice that with all of these instruction groups the various addressing modes which are available for that particular microprocessor can be applied, e.g. the LOAD instruction can be applied in most microprocessors with Direct, Indirect and Immediate Addressing options.

2.14 MICROPROCESSOR SURVEY

2.14.1 4-bit microprocessors

The most common range of 4-bit microprocessors is the Texas Instruments TMS 1000 family. The entire microcomputer is assembled on a single chip. A typical chip in this range includes a

CPU, 1K bytes of ROM for program, sixty-four 4-bit words of RAM for data and input/output facilities for 8 or 16 signals.

2.14.2 8-bit microprocessors

These microprocessors are the most widely applied in applications which require more computing power than the simple 4-bit machines can offer. They use N-MOS technology in place of P-MOS and consequently are approximately 10 times faster. The main types are:

INTEL 8080. This requires three chips—the clock generator, the CPU itself and the system controller. It was the first mass-produced 8-bit microprocessor.

INTEL 8085. This packs the CPU and system controller of the 8080 onto a single chip. It possesses a few additional instructions and a more powerful interrupt system compared with the 8080, but was designed so that programs written on the 8080 would run on the 8085. It possesses the unusual feature of multiplexing its Data Bus with one-half of the Address Bus.

ZILOG Z80. This device was designed by a breakaway team from the original Intel 8080 design group and is a more powerful microprocessor than the 8080 and 8085. It has two complete sets of registers and possesses relative and indexed addressing (not available on the Intel devices). Additionally instructions were added to enable single bits in a register to be tested and to cause block transfers of data around memory.

MOTOROLA 6800. This device has two accumulators but no general-purpose registers. Thus it must use RAM for much data storage. It possesses relative and indexed addressing. It is similar in power to the 8085.

MOS TECHNOLOGY 6502. This device is fairly similar to the 6800. Whilst normally packaged in the usual 40-pin package it has a cheaper reduced version in a 28-pin package.

2.14.3 16-bit microprocessors

16-bit microprocessors perform arithmetic far faster than 8-bit microprocessors and are a major improvement over their predecessors. They are better suited to "number-crunching" applications and are approaching minicomputers in terms of computing power. They offer more addressing modes than 8-bit processors. The main types are:

INTEL 8086. This has fourteen 16-bit registers and eight of these registers are so general-purpose that they can be considered to be Accumulators. It has a wide range of addressing modes and is well supported by control and input/output devices, e.g. the 8089 input/output chip is in fact based on a 8080 microprocessor. The 8088 is the second 16-bit microprocessor which Intel have added to their range.

ZILOG 8001. This has sixteen 16-bit registers and has the facility of combining registers to provide 32-bit and even 64-bit register operation. At first sight it appears to have less addressing modes than other processors. However, some addressing modes are included in the instruction set. Its interrupt vectors can be located anywhere in memory.

MOTOROLA 68000. This processor has the most impressive set of registers—fifteen 32-bit. However, it should not be defined as a 32-bit microprocessor because data is moved around the CPU in 16-bit modules. It has the usual range of addressing modes and has been designed so that the existing range of 6800 support chips can be used (in pairs).

NATIONAL SEMICONDUCTOR 16000. This processor possesses eight 32-bit registers and the most recent ideas for extended addressing (e.g. backing store addresses extend past ROM/RAM addresses). Its interrupt vectors can be located anywhere in memory.

TEXAS 9900. This microprocessor is really a minicomputer designed onto a single chip. It has no on-chip work registers; these are held in RAM. Thus it is slower than all the other processors. However, it possesses an extremely powerful interrupt handling capability. When an interrupt occurs, it does not have to store its registers; it simply switches to a second set elsewhere in the memory.

FERRANTI F100L. This is the only British microprocessor to date. It is currently used for military applications only but will probably be released for general use later.

It should be noted that memory systems used by these processors are 8-bit. Therefore these 16-bit microprocessors require two memory locations/addresses for each instruction.

All of these 16-bit processors are N-MOS devices. To save pin space three of them (8086, 1600 and 8001) multiplex the Address and Data Buses.

It is worthwhile summarising a comparison of microprocessors by saying that no one device is clearly the most powerful or the "best buy". Almost any one of them can be made to perform almost any function. Therefore the best choice is normally the one that is available.

FURTHER READING

1. Woollard, B.G., *Digital Integrated Circuits and Computers,* McGraw Hill, New York and London, 1980.
2. Osborne, A., *An Introduction to Microcomputers,* Vol. 1, Osborne and Associates, New York, 1977.

Chapter 3

Plant Measurements and Microcomputer Interface

3.1 INTRODUCTION

To perform plant monitoring and control by microcomputer an electrical interface with the plant must be created. Plant parameters must be measured and an indication of significant plant events recorded. These must be converted into electrical analogue (continuous) signals or digital (on/off) signals. On a smaller scale the plant measurement and control equipment must receive output signals from the microcomputer for control purposes, e.g. control loop settings, interlocks or start/stop signals.

A general description of the role of the plant interface is shown in Figure 3.1. Input/Output modules within the microcomputer drive the plant interface. This is simply an assembly point for a multiplicity of different types of analogue and digital signals. Sometimes it will in-

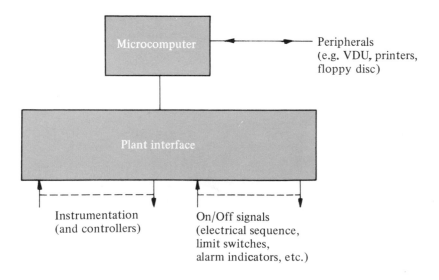

FIGURE 3.1 THE ROLE OF THE PLANT INTERFACE

clude signal conversion equipment for both analogue and digital input/output signals to enable correct electrical interfacing between computer and plant equipment.

In most applications a microcomputer is interfaced to an established plant with existing instrumentation and electrical control equipment. Clearly this raises the problem of signal compatibility, and signal conversion equipment or replacement transducer/ measurement equipment may have to be installed.

In this chapter the following main elements in the plant measurement and computer interface system are described:

TRANSDUCERS. Measuring techniques for temperature, flow, pressure, level, weight, chemical analysis and miscellaneous requirements are listed in sections 3.2 to 3.8. These lists are clearly not exhaustive and summarise the most common types.

ANALOGUE INPUTS. These signals are generated by the transducer just described and signal ranges are discussed in section 3.9.

DIGITAL INPUTS. Types are discussed in section 3.10.

ANALOGUE OUTPUTS. Types and uses are discussed in section 3.11.

DIGITAL OUTPUTS. Types are discussed in section 3.12.

ADDITIONAL REQUIREMENTS. Sections 3.13 to 3.17 describe amplification techniques and other signal processing, installation details and typical plant interfaces. The microcomputer scanning, A/D and D/A equipment are described separately in Chapter 4.

3.2 TEMPERATURE MEASUREMENT

3.2.1 Thermocouple

The principle of operation of a thermocouple is that a small voltage is generated across one junction of a pair of dissimilar metals when that junction is heated and the other junction is kept cool.

Figure 3.2 shows the connection arrangement from thermocouple tip A to measuring instrument F (amplifier and indicator/recorder/ computer interface). The thermocouple leads B and C are connected to the connecting wires D and E. D and E should be made of the same

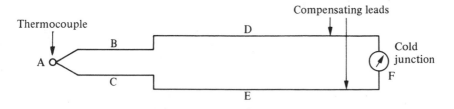

FIGURE 3.2 THERMOCOUPLE CIRCUIT

material as B and C except in the case of rare-metal thermocouples where the expense of long connecting leads would be prohibitive. Leads of copper and copper–nickel alloy are commonly substituted for D and E in this situation. This is commonly called "compensating cable".

Table 3.1 lists the main features of common thermocouples.

TABLE 3.1 THERMOCOUPLE TYPES

Positive wire	Negative wire	Recommended max. working temp.		Voltage at max. continuous working temp.
		Spot	Continuous	
RARE METAL GROUP				
90% Plat, 10% RH	Platinum	1600°C	1400°C	14.33 mV
87% Plat, 13% RH	Rhodium	1600°C	1400°C	16.04 mV
BASE METAL GROUP				
Copper	Constantan	500°C	400°C	20.68 mV
Iron	Constantan	1100°C	850°C	47.39 mV
Chromel	Alumel	1300°C	1100°C	45.14 mV

A difficulty with thermocouple measurement is that the generated voltage is not linear with temperature rise.

3.2.2 Resistance thermometer

The principle of operation of a resistance thermometer is that the electrical resistance of a conducting wire varies with temperature. The measuring resistor invariably takes the form of a coil of wire wound on a former and this is connected to one arm of a Wheatstone bridge. The out-of-balance voltage in the bridge can then be amplified to drive an indicator/recorder/computer interface.

Two materials are used in the manufacture of these devices: platinum gives a normal maximum temperature of 540°C and nickel gives a figure of 300°C.

3.2.3 Radiation pyrometers

Radiation pyrometers use the emission of radiant energy from the hot body as the means of measurement. They are used for measuring temperatures which are higher than can be handled by thermocouples, or for measuring objects in inaccessible positions.

A Total Radiation Pyrometer is shown in Figure 3.2b. Radiation of all wavelengths is focused by a lens or concave mirror onto a thermopile. This is simply a radial assembly of minute thermocouples which are wired in series to sum the emfs generated. Thereafter the signal is handled in the same manner as a thermocouple.

An alternative device is the Optical Pyrometer, which measures just one part of the radiation spectrum, the visible region. However, this instrument is manual in operation and its non-continuous indicating feature makes it unsuitable for computer interfacing.

A final and more convenient type of pyrometer is the Light-sensitive Cell Pyrometer. These instruments make use of photo-conductive and photoelectric (generates emf) principles and use similar focusing techniques to those described above.

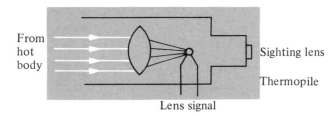

FIGURE 3.2(b) TOTAL RADIATION PYROMETER

3.2.4 LED and photodetector

A recent and novel technique is shown in Figure 3.3. A LED (light-emitting diode) is firmly attached to the hot body. The device uses the principle that light emitted from a conducting LED decreases with increasing temperature. The photo-detector measures the amount of light emitted.

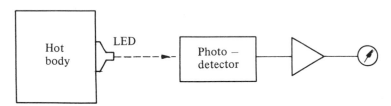

FIGURE 3.3 LED AND PHOTODETECTOR TEMPERATURE MEASUREMENT

3.3 FLOW MEASUREMENT

3.3.1 Differential pressure meters

Differential Pressure Meters use the principle that the pressure difference between measuring points before and after an obstruction to the fluid flow is related to the flow rate.

Figure 3.4 shows perhaps the most common device—the Orifice Plate.

Figure 3.5 shows a Venturi Tube which produces a lower pressure drop than an Orifice Plate but which requires a much longer length of pipe, e.g. 7 ft long for a 10-in. pipe.

Figure 3.6 shows a nozzle which is often used in place of the simpler Orifice Plate for high-velocity flows.

Figure 3.7 shows a Pitot Tube.

In these instruments the flow is proportional to the square root of the differential pressure.

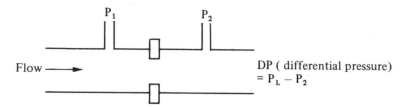

FIGURE 3.4 FLOW (DP) MEASUREMENT BY ORIFICE PLATE

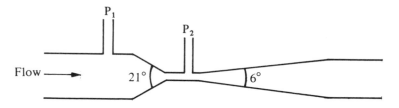

FIGURE 3.5 FLOW (DP) MEASUREMENT BY VENTURI TUBE

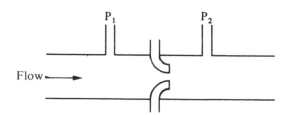

FIGURE 3.6 FLOW (DP) MEASUREMENT BY NOZZLE

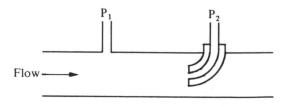

FIGURE 3.7 FLOW (DP) MEASUREMENT BY PITOT TUBE

3.3.2 Area meter

Area Meters are often known by their trade names of Rotameters (in Britain) and Flowrators (in America). A float is supported in a vertical flow of gas or fluid up through a tapered tube and the rate determines the annular area which is formed by the space between the float and the wall of the pipe. The vertical position of the float is thus a measure of flow. Indication of flow rate can be obtained by mechanical linkage to the float stem or by the use of a magnetic follower (external magnetic follower tracks movement of float).

3.3.3 Miscellaneous techniques

Many other less frequently applied techniques for flow measurement exist.

One example is the Anemometer, which is basically a velocity-measuring instrument. A circular vane or cup assembly is allowed to rotate in the air or gas flow and the rotational speed is taken as a measure of flow.

In the Magnetic Flowmeter the fluid, which must be electrically conducting, flows through a magnetic field. Two electrodes are mounted in the fluid, and the conductivity between them is a measure of flow. This device has the advantage that there is no pressure drop across the detecting element (cf. orifice plate).

3.4 PRESSURE MEASUREMENT

3.4.1 Bourdon tube

The Bourdon Tube represents a very ubiquitous mechanical tool, and it consists of a metal tube of approximately elliptical cross-section. The tube is shaped into one of three forms: C-shape, spiral or helix, as shown in Figure 3.8. When pressure is applied to the device the tube tends to straighten and movement of the free end is used to give indication.

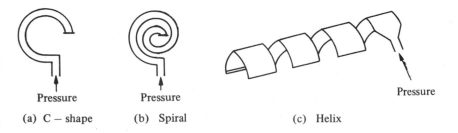

(a) C – shape   (b) Spiral   (c) Helix

FIGURE 3.8 BOURDON TUBE FOR PRESSURE MEASUREMENT

3.4.2 Manometer

The Manometer, or U-tube, is probably the most familiar pressure measuring technique. Frequently one limb is much wider and shorter than the other, and in such cases a float is mounted in the wide chamber. The float is then mechanically linked through a pressure-tight seal, to operate a pen or pointer (again possibly with a signal drive to a computer interface).

Several variations of the simple Manometer exist. One such device is the Ring Balance, which is shown in Figure 3.9. If pressure P_2 is greater than pressure P_1 the ring rotates about its pivoted centre until the opposing moment, which is created by counter weight M, balances the rotating moment. Notice that this instrument measures the difference between P_1 and P_2. Thus it can be used for measurement of:

(a) Gauge pressure—if either P_1 or P_2 is atmospheric pressure.

(b) Absolute pressure—if either P_1 or P_2 is fed from a vacuum (zero pressure).

(c) Differential pressure—flow can be measured using this device. This is a common feature with many pressure measuring devices; they can be used for pressure, flow and even level measurement, e.g. the manometer. Temperature can also be measured with some devices, e.g. the expansion of a sealed bellows.

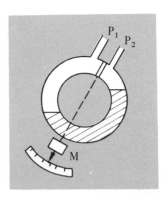

FIGURE 3.9 RING BALANCE FOR PRESSURE MEASUREMENT

3.4.3 Diaphragm/Bellows

The principle of a diaphragm, or its more complex assembly—the bellows, is shown in Figure 3.10. Materials used are flexible rubber, synthetic plastic or metal.

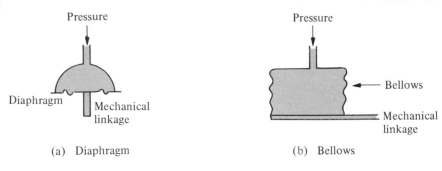

(a) Diaphragm   (b) Bellows

FIGURE 3.10 DIAPHRAGM/BELLOWS FOR PRESSURE MEASUREMENT

3.5 LEVEL MEASUREMENT

3.5.1 Float-operated devices

A typical float-operated level measuring system is shown in Figure 3.11. The cord and pulley system could be replaced by a direct drive through a stuffing gland in the wall of the tank to an electrical potentiometer. Alternatively the cord could drive a Selsyn (or "Magslip") synchro transmitter for remote transmission to a synchro receiver which rotates in unison with the transmitter.

A variation on the float arrangement is the Buoyancy Gauge. In this device the displacer (buoy in place of float) is heavier than the fluid. However, it is prevented from sinking by means of a vertical support. This support is mechanically linked (often with a torque tube) to the indicating/recording/transmission device. The advantage of this device over the float is that for a long displacer a much smaller vertical movement is caused for tank empty to tank full.

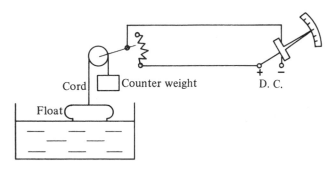

FIGURE 3.11 FLOAT DEVICE FOR LEVEL MEASUREMENT

3.5.2 Electrical devices

Electrical devices use the dielectric (for capacitance) and conductivity properties of the fluid to produce level measurement.

Figure 3.12 shows the arrangement for a Capacitor Gauge and a Conductivity Gauge. In the former case the capacitance is at a minimum when the level is low. Similarly the electrical conductivity in the second case is at a minimum when the tank is empty.

Both transducers feed to a.c. bridges rather than d.c. bridges to avoid electrolysis of the liquid in the tank.

These devices can be used for very large movements of level (over 100 ft).

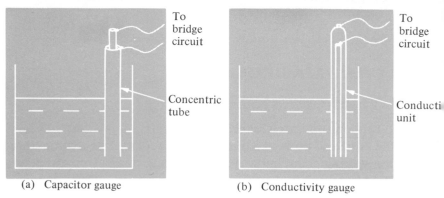

(a) Capacitor gauge   (b) Conductivity gauge

FIGURE 3.12 ELECTRICAL DEVICES FOR LEVEL MEASUREMENT

3.5.3 Pressure devices

The principle of operation of pressure devices for level measurement is that the pressure at the bottom of a tank is a measure of the liquid level in the tank.

Many measuring devices are applied—manometer, diaphragm, bellows, air capsule.

3.5.4 Radiation

Radiation devices do not require contact with the measured liquid.

Figure 3.13 shows how gamma radiation is directed through the liquid. The absorption of gamma radiation in the measuring cell is a function of the mass of the intervening liquid/solid.

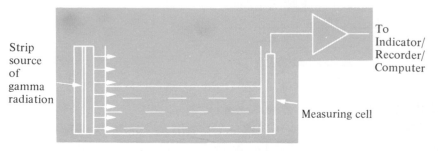

FIGURE 3.13 RADIATION DEVICE FOR LEVEL MEASUREMENT

3.5.5 Ultrasonic sensor

The Ultrasonic Sensor shown in Figure 3.14 uses the same principle as a ship's echo-sounder for detecting fish, submarines or sea-bed. The time difference between the transmission and reception of a pulsed sound beam is a measure of depth or level.

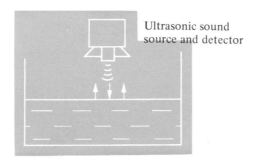

Ultrasonic sound source and detector

FIGURE 3.14 ULTRASONIC SENSOR FOR LEVEL MEASUREMENT

3.6 WEIGHT MEASUREMENT

3.6.1 Electrical-resistance strain gauges

When an electrical conductor is strained, its resistance changes. A typical Electrical-resistance Strain Gauge is shown in Figure 3.15. The metal foil (occasionally wire) is arranged in a grid pattern and is mounted on a backing material. The assembled gauge is bonded with a suitable adhesive to a convenient surface of the load-bearing assembly and covered with a protective wax or lacquer. It is connected to a Wheatstone bridge.

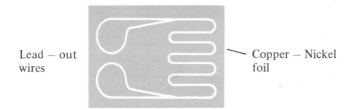

Lead – out wires

Copper – Nickel foil

FIGURE 3.15 ELECTRICAL RESISTANCE STRAIN GAUGE

Figure 3.16 shows how a second "dummy" strain gauge can be added to the bridge circuit to provide temperature compensation. Frequently all arms of the bridge can be made "active" such that four strain gauges mounted in appropriate positions on the load-bearing assembly can combine to produce a larger unbalance signal.

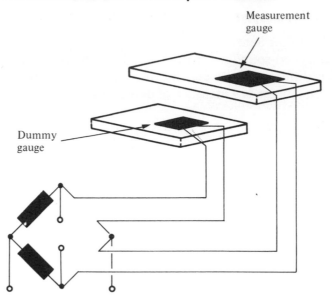

FIGURE 3.16 TEMPERATURE-COMPENSATING WHEATSTONE BRIDGE

3.6.2 Semiconductor strain gauges

A Semiconductor Strain Gauge construction is shown in Figure 3.17. The piezo-resistance effect of silicon is utilised such that a dimensional change causes a resistance or conductivity change. The Wheatstone Bridge circuit is again normally applied.

Such devices produce outputs which are far greater than for electrical-resistance gauges, but they are less accurate and more temperature sensitive. An assembly of strain gauges which is designed to support the load-bearing structure is commonly termed a "loadcell".

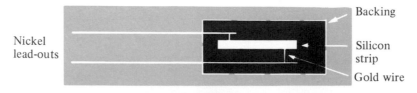

FIGURE 3.17 SEMICONDUCTOR STRAIN GAUGE

3.6.3 Other strain gauges

Whilst the devices described above dominate applications, occasionally other techniques are applied.

A piezoelectric crystal will suffer an electric charge when strained. The sensitivity of a transducer based on this principle is far higher than for the conductivity devices described above, but stability is poor.

The varying magnetic permeability of a strained material is used with magnetostrictive transducers.

In another device the frequency of vibration of a stretched wire is used to indicate strain on the wire mounting.

3.7 CHEMICAL ANALYSIS

3.7.1 Infra-red analysis (gas)

Infra-red analysers are commonly used for providing continuous gas analysis for constituents such as CO, CO_2 and H_2.

Figure 3.18 shows the method of operation for a single constituent. Infra-red radiation is directed through the sampled gas stream to an infra-red detector. The detector is a chamber which is filled with the same gas as that which is being measured. The rate of radiation absorption is varied by changing the concentration of the measured gas constituent. The temperature of the detecting chamber is measured by a thermocouple or expansion of the chamber is used to deflect a diaphragm.

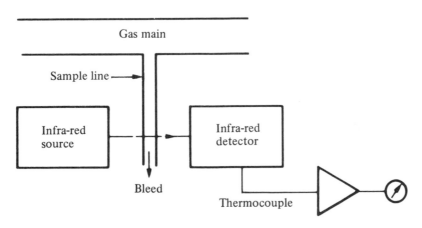

FIGURE 3.18 INFRA-RED GAS ANALYSER

3.7.2 Ionisation chamber (gas)

Figure 3.19 shows an Ionisation Chamber in which a radium source of alpha particles is used to ionise the gas within it. The content of the gas under measurement varies the conductivity between the two electrodes by immobilising the electrons formed by ionisation. The current flow is then a measure of gas concentration.

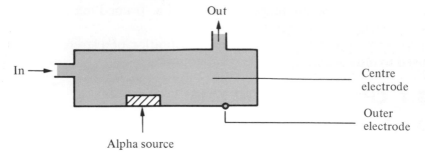

FIGURE 3.19 IONISATION CHAMBER GAS ANALYSER

3.7.3 Paramagnetic analysis (gas)

These analysers are only used for oxygen measurement since no other gas is sufficiently paramagnetic (attracted by a magnetic field). In such an analyser the intensity of flow caused by a steady magnetic field is governed by the concentration of oxygen in the sample. Figure 3.20 shows how this varying flow is detected by the cooling effect on a heated element placed in the accelerated gas stream.

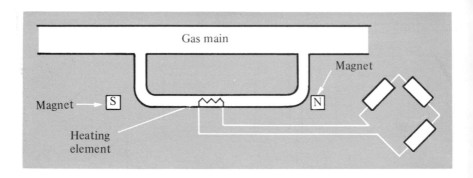

FIGURE 3.20 PARAMAGNETIC ANALYSER (FOR OXYGEN)

3.7.4 Thermal conductivity analysers (gas)

In these devices the gas flows around an electrically heated element which forms one arm of a Wheatstone bridge. The flow is maintained constant as shown in Figure 3.21 so that if any variation occurs in the concentration of the constituent under measurement then the thermal conductivity of the gas stream will vary.

Thus the temperature of the heating element and hence its resistance vary accordingly. Correction must be made for variation of the other gas constituents.

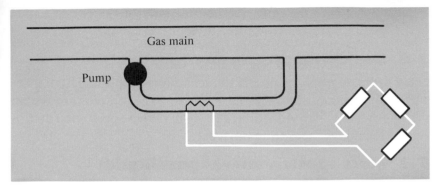

FIGURE 3.21 THERMAL CONDUCTIVITY GAS ANALYSER

3.7.5 Humidity measurement (gas)

There are a multiplicity of techniques for measuring humidity, or moisture content, of a gas.

An Assman's Hygrometer, or "wet and dry bulb" arrangement, is shown in Figure 3.22. A moistened wick is wrapped around the wet bulb and water evaporates from this wick into the gas (normally air). This cools the wet bulb, and the rate of evaporation is determined by the humidity of the gas/air. The wet bulb depression is thus an indication of humidity. Thermocouples could replace the wet and dry bulbs.

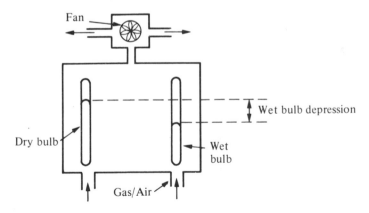

FIGURE 3.22 ASSMAN'S HYGROMETER FOR HUMIDITY MEASUREMENT

An alternative device is the Dew Cell, or Lithium Chloride Cell. This uses lithium chloride crystals, which are deliquescent, i.e. absorb or give up water to the atmosphere until a state of equilibrium is reached. The degree of absorption is governed by the amount of moisture present in the atmosphere. Lengths of fabric are immersed in solutions of lithium chloride (calcium chloride is a substitute) and after drying the compound crystallises on to the fabric. When an a.c.

voltage is applied to the unit, the conductivity of the circuit varies with moisture absorption from the atmosphere.

3.7.6 Gas chromatography (gas)

Gas Chromatography is simply the technique of splitting a complex gas flow into its constituent gases by passing the stream through an absorbing column. The individual gases will then be presented in turn to one of the above measuring devices.

3.7.7 Mass spectrometer (gas/liquid)

The Mass Spectrometer is commonly used in petrochemical work for analysis of hydrocarbons, e.g. methane, ethane, propane, butane, naphtha, paraffin, etc. The instrument does not give continuous readings for gas/liquid; indeed the complete analysis may take an hour or more. Thus a mass spectrometer is not commonly interfaced to a computer for plant monitoring or control purposes. The device uses the principle that ionised particles of the various elements/compounds in the gas/liquid are deflected by varying amounts in a magnetic field.

3.7.8 Analysis of solid materials

Analysis of solid materials once again is a discontinuous process. However, computers are commonly used to assist the analysis.

Figure 3.23 illustrates the method of operation for two similar types of analysers, one for metallic materials and the other for non-metallic materials. For the former a high-voltage spark is applied to a carefully machined sample, and the radiation produced is deflected and detected. X-rays are applied to non-metallic samples in the latter category and the deflection and detection techniques are similar.

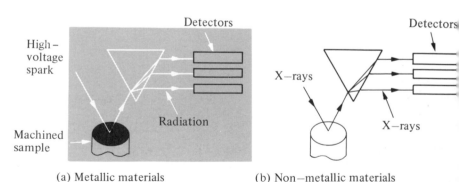

(a) Metallic materials   (b) Non-metallic materials

FIGURE 3.23 ANALYSIS OF SOLID MATERIALS

3.8 MISCELLANEOUS MEASUREMENTS

The categories of measuring transducers described above include the great majority of plant measurements which are required for plant monitoring and control purposes.

Occasionally it is required to measure the speed of rotation of a piece of machinery, e.g. a fan or motor. The standard device which is used for this measurement is the tachogenerator. The "tacho" is mechanically linked to the rotating shaft and produces a d.c. voltage which is proportional to the speed of rotation.

The thickness or "gauge" of a material is frequently measured, e.g. steel strip. An X-ray gauge can be used for this purpose. An X-ray source is sited on one side of the material and the thickness of the material attenuates the quantity of X-rays which fall on the detector on the other side.

Other measuring devices exist for detecting angle, position, force, vibration, pH, power factor and power.

3.9 SIGNAL RANGES

Instrument systems which use the devices described above are often little more than a transducer which feeds directly to a local indicator. The drive can be electrical, pneumatic, mechanical or hydraulic. Often amplification and other signal processing is necessary for driving to a remote indicator, recorder, 3-term controller or computer interface.

There have been several standard instrument signal ranges which have been selected so that equipment from different manufacturers can be directly linked, e.g. a transducer feeding an electrical signal to a chart recorder.

There are several standard ranges in use for electrical signals which represent "analogue" readings. The most common are:

(a) 0–10 mA,
(b) 0–10 V,
(c) 4–20 mA.

(a) and (b) are similar in that (a) can be simply converted to (b) by terminating the 0–10 mA signal in a precision resistance of 1 kΩ.

(a) and (c) are termed "current loop" and drive a current of a particular value through a circuit of any (within reason) resistance value. Thus if an instrument delivers a reading of 6 mA for type (a), 6 mA will flow in a circuit of 500 kΩ, 1 kΩ or whatever. The generating circuit achieves this because it possesses a high input resistance.

Type (c) is a more recent standard and has the particular advantage of possessing a "live zero". 4 mA flows when the transducer reading is zero and this is particularly useful for fault finding because the detection of a 4-mA quiescent signal proves circuit continuity, power-supply operation, etc. The absence of the 4-mA base signal can also be used to indicate failure/alarm conditions.

Pneumatic measuring systems possess a more universal standard of 3–15 psig, which has even survived metrication. Notice the "live zero" feature. Pneumatic to electrical signal conversion (and vice versa) is often necessary, e.g. for computer interfacing. One type of P–E (pneumatic to electric) converter is shown in Figure 3.24. The pneumatic input pressure changes cause movement to the bellows. Mechanical linkage causes the differential transformer former to move, thus varying the secondary voltages E_1 and E_2. The difference between E_1 and E_2 is then the electrical output of the converter. An E–P (electric to pneumatic) converter operates using similar principles. Notice that a "balanced" signal has neither of its signal wire connections connected to the system 0 V, whilst an "unbalanced" signal has one connection connected to 0 V.

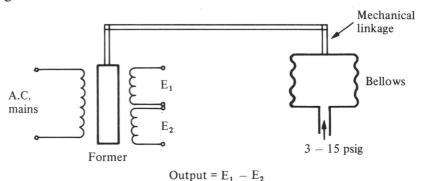

Output = $E_1 - E_2$

FIGURE 3.24 P-E CONVERTED

3.10 DIGITAL INPUTS

Digital input (or on/off) signals are easier to generate from a plant and easier to handle. They are more rugged in the sense that a signal is either there or not there, and electrical noise problems and poor earthing arrangements are less likely to cause errors compared with analogue inputs (which have just been described).

Two types of signal can be used:

(a) Voltage, e.g. +12 V and 0 V, to represent plant or equipment condition.

(b) Contact Closure, i.e. open-circuit or short-circuit.

The latter is by far the most common. It avoids signal-handling difficulties if voltage signals are being generated from several different types of electrical or electronic equipment which operate at different voltage levels. It allows the computer input equipment to transform the contact closure into whatever signal level it requires, e.g. by driving a current through the contact, or using a "pull-up" resistor to set the signal to a standard voltage level. Sometimes voltage levels are not available at remote equipment, e.g. a mechanically triggered limit switch; this is simply handled as a contact closure. Additionally the use of contact-closure signals more readily allows "multiplexing" of digital inputs to occur—this will be described in the next chapter.

Types of digital input signals are:

(i) RELAY CONTACTS. There are often spare contacts on relays which have other primary functions, e.g. manual switching on a piece of equipment, activating a solenoid, closing a valve, starting a motor—in this latter case the relay may be a heavy-duty contactor which presents difficulties with slow contact "bounce". Signals may be produced by dedicated relays, e.g. an instrument may provide the computer with contact-closure signals to indicate "instrument calibrating" or "reading in alarm" through specially installed relays.

(ii) PUSHBUTTONS. It is often useful for the computer to detect the operation of particular manual-operated pushbuttons or switches. These may represent emergency actions such as stop, or regular events during manual operation of the process, e.g. dispense additive, start conveyor. Often the contact closure for such signals may be supplied by a second contact on an existing switch or pushbutton. Frequently a complete dedicated keyboard panel may be required for the operator to enter data to the computer. The pressing of any key is read by the computer as a contact closure.

Within this category we should include "unusual" switches which are read in the same way. Examples are rotary or thumbwheel switches.

(iii) LIMIT SWITCHES. Limit or microswitches can be set by mechanical movement to indicate the location or position of plant or machinery, e.g. charging car positioned beneath a particular material bunker, hoist system in normal position.

(iv) CAMS. Eccentric cams are sometimes added to shaft couplings so that a switched contact can be set to indicate the rotary position of the shaft, e.g. vessel-tilt position.

(v) TRANSISTOR DRIVES. Occasionally electronic equipment, which is to interface with a computer, will present digital input signals at the voltage levels determined by the d.c. power rail within the equipment. This may be the standard TTL levels of $+5$ V and 0 V, or

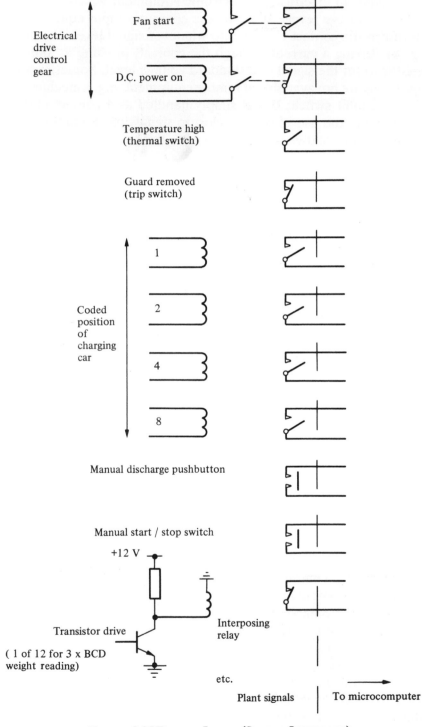

FIGURE 3.25 DIGITAL INPUTS (SAMPLE INTERFACE)

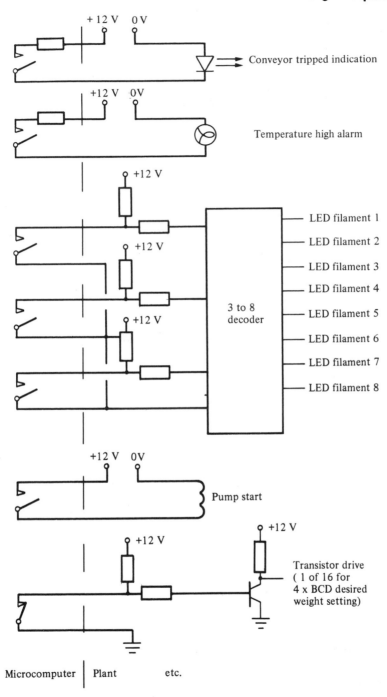

Conveyor tripped indication

Temperature high alarm

+12 V

LED filament 1

+12 V

LED filament 2

LED filament 3

LED filament 4

3 to 8
decoder

LED filament 5

+12 V

LED filament 6

LED filament 7

LED filament 8

+12 V 0V

Pump start

+12 V

+12 V

Transistor drive
(1 of 16 for
4 x BCD desired
weight setting)

Microcomputer | Plant   etc.

FIGURE 3.26 DIGITAL OUTPUTS (SAMPLE INTERFACE)

perhaps +12 V and 0 V. Clearly these signals cannot be treated as contact closures and either special computer input circuitry or interposing relays will have to be applied.

When contact bounce occurs, particularly with types (i) and (ii) (relay contacts and pushbuttons), special measures may have to be taken to prevent the computer reading two or more operations of the signal. This can be done by hardware, i.e. by quenching any bounce in the relay contact circuit itself by means of a capacitor, or by software, i.e. by computer program scanning at a lower frequency or by ignoring subsequent setting of the signal until a minimum time has elapsed.

A typical digital input interface looks like Figure 3.25. In this hypothetical configuration a mixture of contact closure signals from electrical drive gear, limit/trip switches, specially designed interfaces (coded position, coded weight) and pushbuttons/switches is interfaced to the remote computer.

3.11 ANALOGUE OUTPUTS

Analogue outputs are usually far smaller in numbers than analogue inputs. The two main areas of application are:

(a) Setpoints to 3-term controllers.

(b) Drives to chart recorders (occasionally to a graph plotter).

The signal ranges are the same as for analogue inputs—commonly 4–20 mA or 0–10 V.

Normally, if a microcomputer application does not possess direct-control facilities, there are no analogue outputs in the configuration.

3.12 DIGITAL OUTPUTS

The most convenient signal type for digital output is contact closure. This enables signal level setting to be performed at the remote device or on the output side of the computer's drive circuitry.

Digital outputs are commonly used for:

(a) Indicators/alarms, e.g. LED or filament lamp to indicate plant/equipment state or emergency condition (LED/lamp may well be flashed in this latter case).

(b) Numerical displays, e.g. LED, Nixie or similar numerical display. Note that the common LED numerical display is produced by illuminating a combination of filaments to produce the particular digit required.

(c) Relay operation, e.g. for motor/fan/pump start-up, isolating valve operation or "accept" signal to reset some external equipment.

(d) Transistor drives, e.g. remote electronic equipment, requires normal TTL logic levels (+5 V, 0 V) or similar levels; such voltage levels can be "hung on" to the computer's output signal line. A stepper motor drive (simply a series of pulses), comes into this category.

Figure 3.26 shows a typical digital output interface comprising these types of output functions. Notice how a 3-bit code is decoded to drive the individual LED filaments for a single numerical display. Also notice the Pump Start signal which energises a relay in the pump drive circuit. This signal has been chosen to give a normally open contact closure such that in the event of a computer failure, or a failure in the +12 V supply, the pump start signal will go to logical 0 and the pump will stop. It is often useful to consider failure conditions such as this to ensure plant integrity or safety in the event of computer failure. In this way equipment which is activated or held on by the computer can "fail-safe".

It is common to utilise a dual signal Start/Stop arrangement for driving remote equipment in the same manner as a conventional relay-latching circuit. Figure 3.27 shows such a circuit, and the computer-driven equivalent arrangement replaces the Start and Stop pushbuttons with computer-energised contact closures. The main contact (not shown) off RL1 controls the main drive circuit whilst the auxiliary contact RL1/1 latches the circuit when the Start pushbutton is released.

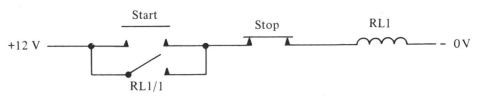

FIGURE 3.27 SELF-LATCHING START/STOP CIRCUIT

Whilst this discussion of digital outputs has been centred around contact-closure signals the use of opto-isolators is increasing. Such a device is shown in Figure 3.28 and has the advantages of small size, reliability and speed of operation. It maintains the same feature of total electrical isolation between plant and computer as for the relay. Opto-isolators can also be used for digital input signals.

3.13 DIGITAL INSTRUMENTATION

One digital instrument which is described frequently in text-books but used rarely is the shaft encoder for indicating rotational position. A 6-bit or 8-bit code is set for the computer to read and decode into angular units.

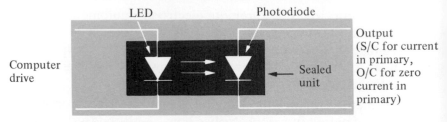

FIGURE 3.28 OPTO-ISOLATOR FOR DIGITAL OUTPUT SIGNAL

Occasionally digital instruments produce a stream of pulses which the computer must handle. Examples are:

(a) Digital tachogenerator.

(b) Weight counters, e.g. 1 pulse for every weight increment.

The microcomputer can handle such signals by software scan or by allowing an interrupt to occur for each pulse. However, the software overhead is often considerable. It is strongly recommended that such signals should be converted in external equipment. An analogue tachogenerator should always be used in preference to a digital tachogenerator (or a frequency to voltage converter should be applied). External counters should be used for pulse streams representing fast events. Such counters would normally then be read in digital form. Note that it is often necessary for the computer to reset (with a digital output signal) a counter of this type.

3.14 AMPLIFIER TECHNIQUES

In this section we consider amplification and signal-processing techniques which are required external to the computer equipment. Any internal amplification of analogue inputs and A/D (analogue to digital) conversion will be considered in the next chapter on Microcomputer System Hardware.

Pneumatic amplification of signals from pneumatic transducers (e.g. bellows, diaphragm) uses the traditional techniques of flapper and nozzle and relay valve. Such devices are beyond the scope of this book but are well documented in traditional instrumentation texts.

It is more worth while to examine electronic amplification techniques, which are based on the Operational Amplifier (op-amp). This device amplifies d.c. and a.c. signals, and its standard symbol is shown in Figure 3.29. In much installed instrumentation it was implemented in discrete component form but is now readily available in integrated circuit form. The most familiar IC op-amp chip is the 741 which is available for a fraction of the price of a discrete component equivalent. The advantages of the IC version include reliability, small size, low cost and less sensitivity to drift caused by temperature changes.

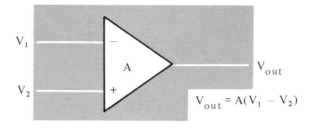

FIGURE 3.29 OPERATIONAL AMPLIFIER SYMBOL

The particular features of the op-amp are:

(a) High input resistance.
(b) High gain.
(c) Low output resistance.
(d) Amplifies d.c. up to 1 MHz or more.
(e) Very little drift due to temperature changes.

Its main design feature is that it is a differential amplifier, i.e. it amplifies only the DIFFERENCE between the two voltages at its input terminals. This is particularly advantageous when an unwanted COMMON MODE signal is present on both input connections. Such a voltage is not amplified giving the amplifier a high "common mode rejection ratio".

Figure 3.30 shows the op-amp connected as a straightforward signal amplifier. The voltage gain is given by:

$$\frac{V_{\text{out}}}{V_{\text{in}}} = -\frac{R_2}{R_1}$$

Thus it is independent of the intrinsic amplifier gain A, which could vary from one device to another. The output is inverted with respect to the input.

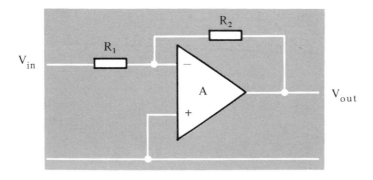

FIGURE 3.30 OP-AMP AS SIMPLE AMPLIFIER

If a non-inverting gain is required the circuit of Figure 3.31 is used.

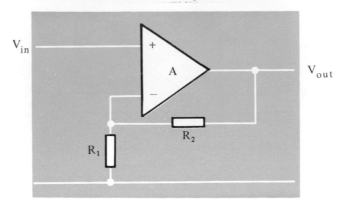

FIGURE 3.31 OP-AMP CIRCUIT TO PRODUCE NON-INVERTING GAIN

Another application of the op-amp is as a comparator. In this case a voltage level (high or low) is set when a signal level is above or below a reference level. The output level can be used to light an alarm indicating lamp/LED or to switch an external device. Figure 3.32 shows the circuit connections. R_2 is chosen to be much larger than R_1, so that a very high gain is applied. Thus when:

$$V_{in} > V_{ref}, V_{out} = -V \text{ (negative saturation)}$$
$$\text{and } V_{in} < V_{ref}, V_{out} = +V \text{ (positive saturation)}.$$

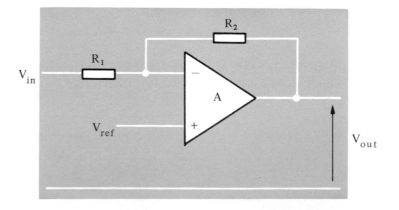

FIGURE 3.32 COMPARATOR CIRCUIT

The op-amp can also be used to add two (or more) signals together in the Summing circuit shown in Figure 3.33. Here:

$$V_{out} = \frac{R_3}{R_1} \times V_1 + \frac{R_3}{R_2} \times V_2$$

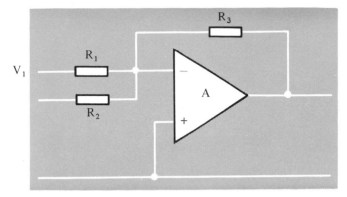

FIGURE 3.33 SUMMING CIRCUIT

More complicated functions can be performed. For example multiplication and even square root extraction can be performed to satisfy the following equation:

$$\text{Flow} = \sqrt[K]{\frac{DP \times P}{T}}$$

DP = differential pressure,
P = pressure,
T = temperature.

Op-amp circuits can be extended to perform linearising, calculations (e.g. integrating, or combining other signals) and smoothing.

In all of these cases it is sometimes advantageous to perform these functions within the microcomputer which logs the signals. These calculations are performed by software when the computer scans the plant interface. The computer can also perform more complex calculations, e.g. operating indices or technical indices for the plant.

Whereas a straightforward thermocouple reading is directly applied to an amplifier (albeit normally with linearising), many electrical transducers feed to a Wheatstone Bridge. These include resistance thermometers, strain gauges, conductivity gauges for level, etc. These bridges are normally of the automatic null-balancing type or, if remote indication or interfacing to a computer is required, of the voltage-sensitive type.

The principle of operation of the automatic null-balancing type is shown in Figure 3.34. A signal for remote indication could be taken off the mechanical linkage which adjusts R_3 to re-balance the bridge. The simpler technique for remote indication or interfacing is the voltage-sensitive bridge shown in Figure 3.35. Here the out-of-balance signal is simply amplified directly. This type of bridge is not as accurate as the null-type.

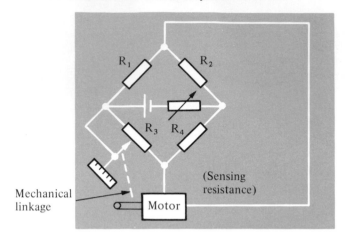

FIGURE 3.34 NULL-TYPE WHEATSTONE BRIDGE

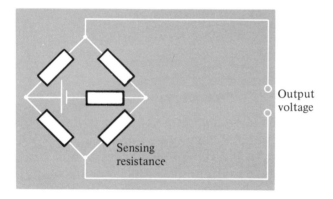

FIGURE 3.35 VOLTAGE SENSITIVE WHEATSTONE BRIDGE

3.15 TYPICAL PLANT INTERFACE

A plant interface to a microcomputer might be a single analogue input plus a single digital input, or it may consist of a few hundred analogue and digital inputs and several dozen outputs.

A simple and hypothetical plant is shown in Figure 3.36. Gas is heated and injected into a liquid mix which is held in a vessel to which batches of solid materials are added. The microcomputer logs a series of instrument readings (analogue) on the gas and vessel, and logs weights (digital) charged from the feed hoppers. It also controls the gas flow, starts the conveyor and opens the hopper gates.

The plant interface might then look like Table 3.2.

TABLE 3.2 PLANT INTERFACE FOR HYPOTHETICAL PLANT

Analogue inputs
   Gas flow
   Gas pressure
   Gas temperature
   Stove temperature
   Mix level
   Vessel weights

Digital inputs
   Hopper weight BCD   1–A
        ,,   B
        ,,   C
        ,,   D
   Hopper weight BCD   2–A
        ,,   B
        ,,   C
        ,,   D
   Hopper weight BCD   3–A
        ,,   B
        ,,   C
        ,,   D
   Hopper 1 Read Demand
    ,,   2 ,,   ,,
    ,,   3 ,,   ,,
   Hopper 1 Gate Open
    ,,   2 ,,   ,,
    ,,   3 ,,   ,,

Analogue outputs
   Gas Flow Setpoint

Digital outputs
   Hopper 1 Accept
    ,,   2   ,,
    ,,   3   ,,
   Discharge Hopper 1 (Open Gate)
        ,,   2   ,,
        ,,   3   ,,
   Start Conveyor
   Stop Conveyor
   Conveyor-stopped Indicator

Notice that the weighing equipment for the three weigh-hoppers feeds a single weight value on a $3 \times$ BCD digital input interface to the computer. The identity of the hopper is given by a simultaneous setting of a single Hopper Read Demand digital input signal. This latter signal will stay set until the computer responds with the appropriate Hopper Accept digital output signal. This technique of employing a response between computer and plant equipment is called "handshaking". Another example of its application is in a situation where an analogue input is discontinuous, e.g. a gas-analysis reading requires some time to become valid. In this case the instrument could generate a digital input "Request Read" signal when the reading is available. The computer would then read the analogue input and reply to, or reset, the Request Read.

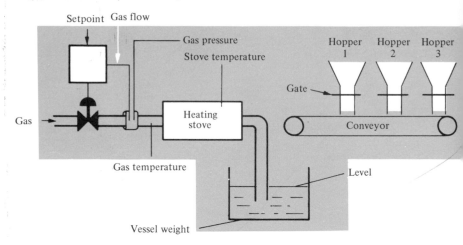

FIGURE 3.36 HYPOTHETICAL PLANT

3.16 INSTALLATION DETAILS

If care is taken with installation of cabling and equipment and correct screening and earthing arrangements are employed, many operating problems with an integrated computer plant logging/control system can be avoided. More faults and inaccuracies are caused by the plant interface than the microcomputer equipment itself.

Figure 3.37 shows how COMMON MODE and SERIES MODE interface signals are generated on plant interfaces. Common Mode signals are voltage levels which exist on both signal lines and are often caused because instrumentation and computer equipment are separated by a long distance and operate at different d.c. voltage levels (with respect to earth); they can also be a.c. voltages. These unwanted signals cannot easily be prevented but they can be overcome by using an amplifier at the receiving end with a high common mode rejection, e.g. an op-amp (see Section 3.14) which amplifies the voltage *difference*.

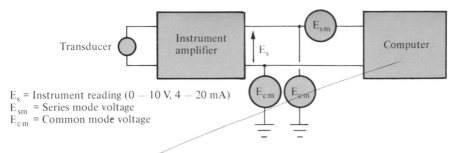

E_s = Instrument reading (0 – 10 V, 4 – 20 mA)
E_{sm} = Series mode voltage
E_{cm} = Common mode voltage

FIGURE 3.37 UNWANTED INTERFERENCE SIGNALS ON INSTRUMENT INTERFACE

Series Mode signals are invariably caused by pick-up of electrical noise on the cable link. Thus often one leg of the signal will exhibit an unwanted a.c. component. This is often 50 Hz a.c. mains pick-up, or occasionally it could be higher frequency signal pick-up, e.g. caused by sparking from a commutator or a piece of r.f. equipment in close proximity. Such interference can be prevented by:

(a) Filtering input signal (i.e. low cut-off frequency in amplifier).
(b) Preventing interference at source.
(c) Separating instrument/computer cables from power cables (separate cable racks).
(d) Using twisted pairs for each signal, and employing screened cable with good earthing arrangements for screens.

Cable screens should never be earthed at more than one point. This can cause "earth loops" and currents may flow in the screens. With large systems which employ many signal cables it is sensible to choose one central marshalling point. At this location signal cable screens should be firmly connected together with heavy-duty cable, e.g. copper braid. This common connection should then be securely wired to a good earth; it may be sensible to excavate and install a deeply embedded ground earth.

It is worth while emphasising the value of selecting good-quality cable and terminations. Cable costs always stagger development staff, but variable voltage drop along low-capacity signal cables and across poor terminal strips can cause lingering problems. There are many terminals manufactured which incorporate facilities for mounting resistors, diodes, fuses and "knife-edge" connectors which ease installation and maintenance functions. Cable cores should always be clamped to spade tips before insertion into terminals; repeated re-moval and re-insertion of a twisted-strand cable will soon cause loose connections due to the tapered shape of the cable core tip. Cable cores, even if coloured, should always be ferruled (i.e. labelled with numbered or lettered collars) so that re-connection mistakes are limited and good cable documentation can be maintained.

3.17 TELEMETRY

When a large number of signals need to be connected to a computer over a long-distance cable costs may become prohibitive. There are two solutions to this problem:

(a) Use distributed processing, i.e. install a signal marshalling microcomputer adjacent to plant and connect by serial link (three or four wires) to centralised computer/microcomputer.

(b) Use a telemetry system. In this approach a telemetry master station is sited at the computer end, and a telemetry outstation is sited at the plant. They are connected by a single cable pair (normally a dedicated telephone pair). The outstation sends a bit pattern of 0s and 1s superimposed on a signal carrier. These 0s and 1s represent both digital inputs and the outputs of A/D converters for analogue instrument signals. The fixed order in which the outstation scans and transmits the plant signals identifies the signals. Data (for digital outputs and analogue outputs) can similarly be transmitted in the opposite direction.

There are two types of telemetry transmission, as follows:

FREQUENCY DIVISION MULTIPLEXING (FDM). Perhaps twenty-four different frequency carriers are scheduled over a frequency range of 0 to 3000 Hz to handle twenty-four digital signals. A 0 or 1 is transmitted as a slightly higher or a slightly lower frequency than the carrier for each signal.

TIME DIVISION MULTIPLEXING (TDM). Large numbers of signals (typically 120) can be transmitted using this method. The technique involves simply transmitting voltage pulses in sequence; the level of each voltage pulse identifies the signal as a 0 or 1. It is even possible to TDM an FDM system, such that on each of 24 FDM frequency carriers, 120 signals can be transmitted sequentially on TDM. Maximum signal capacity is then 2880 (24×120).

FURTHER READING

1. Gregory, B.A., *An Introduction to Electrical Instrumentation*, Macmillan, London, 1975.
2. Jones, E.B., *Instrument Technology*, Vols. 1 and 2, Butterworth, London, 1974.
3. Woolvet, G.A., *Transducers in Digital Systems*, Peter Peregrinus Ltd., Stevenage, 1977.

Chapter 4

Microcomputer System Hardware

4.1 MICROCOMPUTER CONFIGURATION

The CPU, ROM, RAM and input/output chips which form the heart of a microcomputer have been discussed in detail in Chapter 2. Peripherals such as VDUs, printers, floppy discs, etc., and special signal-handling circuitry for analogue and digital inputs and outputs will be described in more detail here.

Microcomputers for plant monitoring and control can vary in size considerably depending upon the application.

A small system which scans a handful of digital input signals (perhaps indicating events in a sequence control application) and a few digital output signals is shown in Figure 4.1. This could handle the start-up sequence for a food-processing plant, a conveyor-control

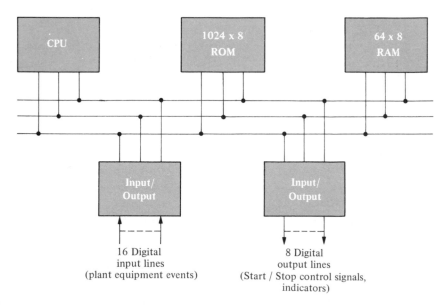

FIGURE 4.1 SMALL PLANT SEQUENCE CONTROL SYSTEM

system or even a traffic-control scheme. The program to perform the sequence is tested and burnt into the ROM on an offline development system and simply plugged or soldered into the board. Notice that there are no operator facilities to monitor the program flow or data in use by means of a keyboard and LED display or by VDU.

A large system which handles several peripherals and a bigger plant interface is shown in Figure 4.2. The TV and keyboard and their interfaces could be replaced with a VDU driven from a Communications Interface. Whilst this system represents a near maximum configuration, it is often sensible to segregate the plant interface into a separate microcomputer in a distributed processing system. This assists development, commissioning and maintenance operations.

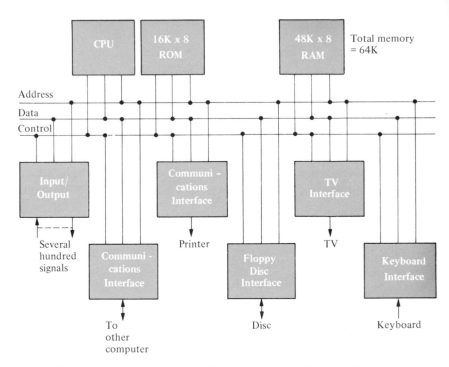

FIGURE 4.2 LARGE PROCESS MONITORING AND CONTROL SCHEME

As microprocessors become more powerful and memory capacity increases, computing power will enable complex multi-function systems to be implemented on microcomputers. Thus an existing minicomputer system consisting of computer, floppy disc, hard disc, several VDUs, several printers, plant interface, communications links to other computers, etc., could be implemented using a microcomputer system. However, the low cost of microcomputer hardware will undoubtedly encourage the application of distributed microcomputer systems in which a network of microcomputers shares the system's facilities.

4.2 STORAGE TECHNIQUES

The floppy disc is a relative newcomer to the computer peripheral market but it is ideally suited to application with microcomputers. It is small and cheap. It forms one of a family of "backing store" devices which provide bulk storage facilities to back-up the computer's main fast store. Backing stores hold programs which are to be loaded into main memory for running in the computer and also data files.

There are two types of fast main store:

(a) Core store, in which bits are held on individual ferrite rings which are magnetised in one direction or another (to indicate 0 or 1).

(b) Semiconductor store, i.e. ROM and RAM, which performs the same function but is faster, consumes less power and is far cheaper than core store.

Whilst semiconductor store is rapidly superseding core store, it should not be forgotten that core store dominated computer memory applications for 20 years and has its own advantages over semiconductor store. It does not lose its bit pattern when switched off as RAM does. Thus RAM always requires reloading after power is lost. Also ROM cannot be written to—core can.

The main types of backing store are:

(i) Magnetic tape, which is extremely slow—the whole tape has to be run before a program at an extreme end of the tape can be read.

(ii) Magnetic drum which is very bulky.

(iii) Magnetic disc which is the most popular device for computers and mainframe computers.

(iv) Floppy disc.

(v) Bubble memory, which consists of a magnetic bubble made on a garnet substrate and is non-mechanical and fast. It is new and may assist semiconductor memory as the main fast memory within the system.

4.3 FLOPPY DISC

The floppy disc is almost universally applied in microcomputers which require bulk storage. Units can handle from 100 K bytes up to 500 K bytes.

The floppy disc itself is literally a disc of flexible material which is coated with a magnetic film; only one side of the disc is normally used. It is permanently packaged inside a paper envelope as shown in Figure 4.3. Two parts of the disc surface are exposed: a centre annulus which is not used for storage, and a section which is viewed through a window cut-out in the paper envelope. It is this section which, as it rotates past the read/write head which is in contact with the moving surface, holds the bit memory pattern.

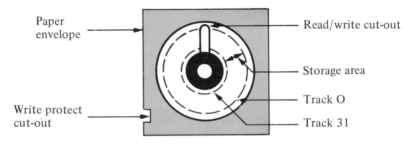

FIGURE 4.3 FLOPPY DISC

The memory area is divided into typically 32 tracks, where each track is represented by a radius of the disc. On each track perhaps sixteen 256-byte sectors/records/blocks are stored.

There are two common sizes for floppy discs:

(a) 8 in. which stores typically 512 K bytes;

(b) 5 in. which stores typically 128 K bytes and is commonly called a "discette".

The centre annulus is gripped by the drive spindle so that the disc rotates inside the paper envelope.

A small cut-out exists in one corner of the envelope. When this is covered (by a sticky label) the disc is "write-protected", i.e. it cannot be written to.

The floppy disc can be easily loaded into and removed from the mechanical drive unit. Care must be taken not to handle the magnetic surface and to protect it from dust.

Just as the microprocessor manufacturers have designed single chips for other input/output and peripheral drive functions to support their CPUs, so have they designed single chips to control a floppy-disc unit. Such chips, or collection of chips for some drive systems, tend to be varied and complex in operation. A block diagram of such a system (which could represent a single chip) is shown in Figure 4.4. The system operates under DMA (direct memory access, or "cycle stealing") so that CPU operation will not be unduly slowed during data transfers.

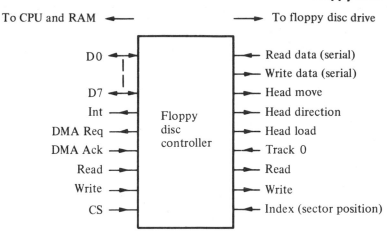

To CPU and RAM ◄——   ——► To floppy disc drive

FIGURE 4.4 FLOPPY DISC CONTROLLER

Information determining track number, sector number (via Data lines) and read or write operation is sent from the CPU to the floppy-disc controller (it can be taken directly from a control block set up in RAM). The controller moves the read/write head (using the Head Move and Head Direction signals) to the required track and compares the required sector address with the actual sector address as the disc rotates. It uses the Index (Sector Position) pulse to trace the actual sector address. When the read/write head is immediately above the demanded position the head is placed in contact with the disc surface using the HEAD LOAD signal and the controller interrupts the CPU. Data is either output from RAM or input from disc to RAM depending on the setting of the READ/WRITE control signals. This data is transferred under DMA control of course, so that DMA Request (the CPUs "Hold" signal) and DMA Acknowledge control signals cause the CPU to pause during byte transfers. The controller "frames" the serial bit patterns read from and written to the disc into bytes for communication to and from RAM.

To avoid over-complexity the address lines which are used to address RAM, which transmits and receives data to and from floppy, are not shown. Indeed they could be set by a separate DMA controller chip.

Information is often stored to the standard IBM 3740 format, which simply requires several bytes of preamble and post-amble data at the start and end of each track.

The floppy disc is an ideal device for transfer of occasional programs and data files. However, a disc is not recommended for more than 40 hours of "Load" activity, i.e. with read/write head actually in contact with the surface. This is not as bad as it first appears, because the head is only in contact with the surface for a few seconds at a time when a transfer takes place. However, it imposes a limitation on an application in which the programming system requires frequent disc transfers, and in these situations the Hard Disc offers itself as a better solution.

4.4 HARD DISC

The Hard Disc gives far longer operational life than a floppy disc, has greater storage capacity and should be more reliable. However it is more expensive.

There are two common types of hard disc:

(a) Removable Disc, which gives the flexibility of allowing the operator or programmer to change "systems", i.e. the programs and data files. Thus a system can be updated by adding new programs (perhaps offline on another machine) to a removable disc. This disc can then be used to replace the operational disc on the online computer; of course the programming system will probably have to be stopped to perform this. There are two types of disc assemblies, as shown in Figure 4.5 In the disc cartridge typically five discs offering ten surfaces (of which only eight are used) are fixed to a common spindle.

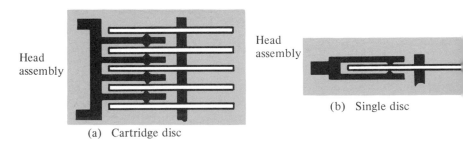

(a) Cartridge disc

(b) Single disc

FIGURE 4.5 DISC ASSEMBLIES

Several read/write heads are required and they move in and out to cover the same track on each surface. The common tracks on each surface combine to produce a "cylinder". A cartridge disc can store from 1 M byte to 100 M bytes and is commonly used with mainframe computers and minicomputers. The simpler single removable disc has a corresponding smaller capacity.

(b) Fixed Disc, which is similar to the single removable disc but its non-removable disc feature makes it cheaper and thus particularly attractive for microcomputer applications. It is useful in powerful microcomputer applications, e.g. development systems, scientific applications and large commercial functions.

A typical read/write head assembly for all types of disc stores is shown in Figure 4.6. Magnetic "spots" are recorded on the disc surface as it passes the Write head; the direction of spot magnetism determines whether a 0 or 1 is stored. In a read operation a small voltage of positive or negative polarity is induced in the Read head to indicate a stored bit.

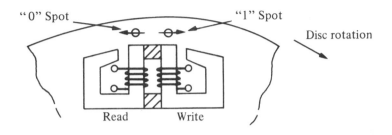

FIGURE 4.6 DISC READ/WRITE HEAD

4.5 MAGNETIC TAPE CASSETTE

Although the domestic audio cassette is rarely used in a real plant application, its use as a convenient and cheap storage medium for programs and data in small personal computers merits a brief description here.

Logical 0s and 1s are normally stored as short bursts (perhaps 2 cycles) of two different frequencies, e.g. 1200 Hz and 2400 Hz. These waveforms are generated simply by a microcomputer program which sets and resets a single digital output line to produce a square wave of the required frequency.

Audio cassettes are extremely slow.

Specially designed magnetic-tape cassettes are commonly used with minicomputers for program storage and are useful devices for applications with microcomputers. The method of bit storage is the same as for disc systems, i.e. magnetic "spots" are polarised in one direction or the other. The read/write head system is also similar. Cassettes of this type are much faster than audio cassettes and can store typically 256 K bytes. However, they are sequential in access, compared with random access for disc systems, and are consequently slower. They are normally only used for program dumping and reload.

4.6 PRINTERS

Printers are used to produce alarm and event messages or production logs in a plant application. They are used in development systems for producing listings of programs.

Invariably they are driven by serial interface, which is described in detail in section 4.10 below.

A line printer is a special type of printer and is not used with microcomputers. It prints a complete line at a time and consequently is exceptionally fast and exceptionally expensive. It is used with mainframe computers.

There are two basic types of printers which are used with minicomputers and microcomputers.

4.6.1 Matrix printer

In this type of printer the character code which is transmitted by the computer is converted into a matrix code for presentation to the printing head.

Figure 4.7 shows a block diagram of a matrix printer. The serial input code is firstly converted to an 8-bit parallel code, possibly in a UART. This code is checked against the codes for the special carriage control codes for "Carriage Return" and "Line Feed". Other special feature codes can also be included, e.g. "Page Format" to shift carriage control to the next page, and "Bell" to sound an alarm bell on the printer.

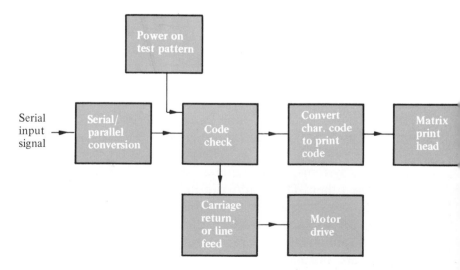

FIGURE 4.7 MATRIX PRINTER BLOCK DIAGRAM

The input character code is then converted to a matrix code in a table look-up ROM and passed to the print head. The head consists of a matrix of tiny solenoid-driven printing needles, typically arranged with seven horizontal rows of needles and nine vertical rows of needles, to produce a 7×9 matrix. Figure 4.8 shows how the matrix block printing head constructs the letter 'A''.

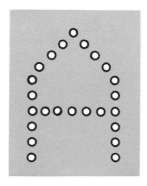

FIGURE 4.8 CONSTRUCTION OF CHARACTER "A" USING MATRIX HEAD

A matrix printer can be extremely fast. A rugged top-quality printer can have the following specification:

(a) 300 characters/second.
(b) Printing on carriage flyback, i.e. prints in both directions.
(c) 256-character buffer store to input characters.
(d) Automatic test pattern on printer when device is switched on; this is produced by an internal microprocessor.
(e) High price! Over £2000. (Slow and light-duty matrix printers are available at a fraction of this cost).

4.6.2 Moving-head printer

A Moving-head printer does not construct its characters using a matrix of dots. It has a print head which supports a discrete printing shape for each character. Consequently it has to rotate, or otherwise reposition its printing head between the printing of adjacent characters. Thus it is significantly slower than a matrix printer. However, its printed text is normally sharper in construction than that of a matrix printer.

Several different types of printing head have been marketed. The most common types are:

(a) The daisy-wheel head, on which the character shapes stand proud of the circumference of a circular rotating head assembly.

(b) The golf-ball head, on which the character shapes are mounted on a spherical head in a row and column arrangement.

With all of these printers the universal code which the computer transmits is ASCII. This is an 8-bit code (7 identifying bits plus 1 parity bit).

4.7 TELEVISION MONITOR

Television receivers are mass-produced and cheap, and for this reason microcomputer manufacturers have designed control chips and circuits which will convert digital patterns held within the microcomputer into video waveforms which can drive domestic television receivers.

The basic principle of operation is shown in Figure 4.9. The electron beam of the television is deflected in the usual manner. The picture information is built up by adding pulses to the video waveform depending on the bit status of RAM (or ROM) byte locations. In the arrangement shown the first 40 bytes of memory store 40×8 screen dots (or "pixels") for the first horizontal scan of the electron beam. The second 40 bytes store the bit pattern for the second line, and so on. Thus for a screen raster of 200 horizontal scans, 200×40 bytes ($= 8000$ bytes) of memory are required.

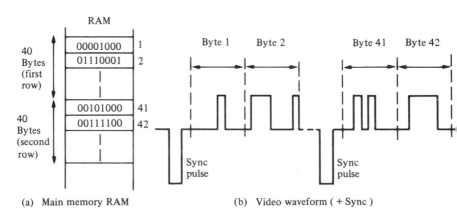

(a) Main memory RAM   (b) Video waveform (+ Sync)

FIGURE 4.9 VIDEO GENERATION

Thus if 8000 memory bytes are assigned to hold the bit coded video information, a DMA output circuit (or chip) can extract this information, build up a composite video plus sync waveform, modulate it onto a R.F. carrier and generate a signal which can be fed directly to the aerial connection of a television receiver. This technique is sometimes called "memory mapped video".

This system enables a totally flexible screen format to be generated, e.g. for detailed graphical displays. However, it is frequently desirable to restrict the display format to a range of symbols, e.g. for text display, and to save considerable computer memory. In this case memory contains text symbol codes (1 code per memory byte). Separate hardware applies a look-up procedure on a ROM which contains complete bit arrays for each text symbol. This is called "character generation". Typically a 40×20 (40 columns, 20 rows) display would require only 800 bytes of memory, although more external character generation hardware is necessary. The character generator ROM for 64 characters and 8 bytes per character would need to be $64 \times 8 = 512$ bytes in size.

In place of output to a domestic television receiver it is often preferred to output the video signal directly to a television monitor, i.e. the composite (video+sync) waveform is applied directly without being modulated onto a R.F. carrier. High-resolution monitors can then be used.

The use of colour television receivers or monitors does not complicate the above description very much. Three colour video signals (R, G and B for red, green and blue) have to be generated in this case. The relative magnitudes of the three signals is determined by the choice of colour. Thus 4 bits are required for each pixel—1 for brightness (dark or light) and 3 for colour code, assuming a total of 8 colours.

4.8 VDU

The VDU (Visual Display Unit) is a stand-alone device which incorporates a display and keyboard. Connection to a computer is by serial link.

The text which is to be displayed is transmitted in ASCII. The video generation techniques which are applied in the VDU are the same as just described. Thus it is in effect a serially-driven television monitor. However, it possesses a keyboard which has the full range of alphanumeric characters.

The VDU is applied when the operator/programmer has to be located away from the microcomputer and when it is more convenient to use a small number of cores in a normal cable (perhaps spare cores in an existing telephone cable). The alternative connection arrangement for a television receiver or monitor of coaxial cable/cables plus separate cable for the keyboard is clearly an inconvenient system for remote devices.

The disadvantages of using a VDU compared with a memory mapped video drive are:

(a) Far slower screen update—typically several seconds for serial-drive VDU compared with instantaneous by DMA-driven video.

(b) Graphs cannot normally be plotted—simulated graphs can be drawn using special character shapes (this is called "semi graphics").

(c) Colour is not normally offered on VDUs.

The advantages of using a VDU can be summarised as:

(a) Can be driven at a distance with small cabling requirements.

(b) Does not tie up DMA memory space.

(c) Several VDUs can be driven conveniently from a single micro-computer.

4.9 KEYBOARDS

At first sight a keyboard, which may consist of more than fifty pushbuttons, presents a large digital input-handling problem. However, specially designed keyboard-control chips and the use of multiplexing enable keyboard inputs to be simple and cheap.

The common method of interfacing a keyboard which is associated with a television receiver is shown in Figure 4.10. For simplicity the diagram shows only three rows and three columns of keys, but in practice at least fifty keys are connected in this type of matrix arrangement (perhaps on a 10×9 basis).

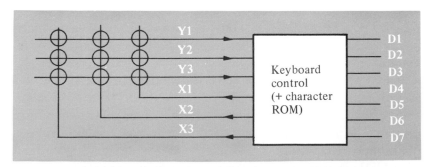

FIGURE 4.10 OPERATION OF KEYBOARD CONTROL CHIP

A single chip, which has its own ROM, sequentially scans columns of keys using pins X1, X2 and X3. It reads in the key settings on Y1, Y2 and Y3. If one key is pressed it generates an appropriate code (stored in ROM) and presents this on the Data Input Highway as D1 to D7.

An alternative and simpler technique is applied in the case of a smaller keyboard plus associated LED segment display, such as is used with cash registers, pocket calculators (normally liquid crystal in place of LED) and single-board microcomputers. The arrangement is shown in Figure 4.11. Two input/output chips are used, and DIGIT 1 to DIGIT 10 output signals are used for both display and keyboard.

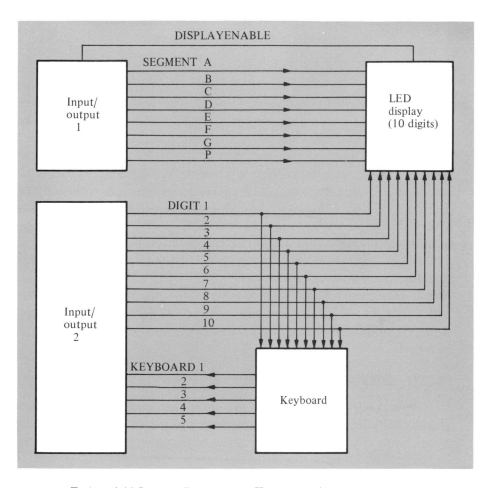

FIGURE 4.11 SHARED DISPLAY AND KEYBOARD ARRANGEMENT

One of ten numerical displays is selected by the setting of one of DIGIT 1 to DIGIT 10. Each digital display consists of seven LED segments, plus a decimal point, as shown in Figure 4.12. The number displayed on the selected display is determined by the setting of SEGMENT A to SEGMENT P. DISPLAYENABLE is the master display control signal which effectively switches on the whole display unit.

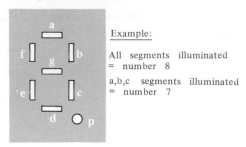

FIGURE 4.12 LED SEGMENT DISPLAY

Program scanning of the keyboard uses the same digital output lines DIGIT 1 to DIGIT 10, but when scanning the keyboard the program must take care not to set DISPLAYENABLE otherwise the display will be activated. The column of keyboard pushbuttons selected by the chosen DIGIT line will then present the settings of that column of 5 keys on the digital input lines KEYBOARD 1 to KEYBOARD 5. The program must scan the entire keyboard (by sequentially setting a DIGIT line and reading the five KEYBOARD lines) fast enough so that it does not miss the pressing of a single key; a sensible scanning speed is every 100 msec.

This method of splitting keyboard pushbutton signals into rows and columns is sometimes called a "matrix" arrangement. The method of sharing the DIGIT lines between display and keyboard is called "multiplexing".

Keyboards which are integrated into a VDU simply transmit serially an ASCII character to the computer whenever a key is pressed.

4.10 GRAPH PLOTTER

Graph Plotters are used to record trends of plant variables, to copy display formats or to plot one parameter against another in a scientific application. They are expensive and not very common.

Drive from computer is either:

(a) Serial, with a fixed character format of X and Y increments; text can also be plotted.

(b) Analogue, with D/A converters supplying the two movements.

4.11 SERIAL TRANSMISSION

Serial transmission is used for printer, VDUs, plotters and data links to other computers.

There are two types of serial data transmission — SYNCHRONOUS and ASYNCHRONOUS.

Synchronous transmission uses data bit transmission which conforms to a precise clock signal. Even when no data is being transmitted, the clock still synchronises the transmit and receive equipment in the two devices. It is used with mainframe computers but is rarely used with microcomputers.

Asynchronous transmission transfers data as soon as the transmission device has data to be sent. Between transmission the transmit and receive devices become passive—they are not under continuous time control. Only asynchronous transmission will be considered from now on.

An international standard for data transmission is applied. This is called V24 or RS-232C and specifies bit patterns, signal level and pin connections.

Figure 4.13 shows the serial bit pattern for a single ASCII character (7 bits) for asynchronous transmission. Normally the signal level is a logical 1 when no transmission is taking place. When a character is transmitted, the signal level is firstly pulsed to logical 0; this is called the Start bit. The 7 data bits are then taken from a parallel/serial converter, which is normally part of a UART, and transmitted with most significant (or left-hand) bit first. Finally a parity bit is sent, and this could be even, odd or "transparent" (not checked) parity. A Stop bit (sometimes two) is then sent whilst the line reverts to its quiescent signal level of logical 1. Further characters can then be transmitted if required.

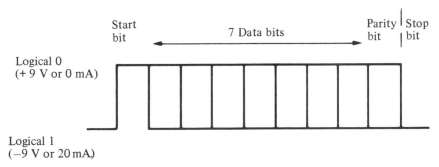

FIGURE 4.13 V24/RS232C SERIAL BIT PATTERN

The duration of each pulse is determined by the transmission speed. This is measured in BAUD (bits per second) and must be precisely set at transmit and receive devices. The standard "baud rates" are 110, 300, 600, 1200, 2400, 4800 and 9600 baud (19200 is occasionally used for inter-computer links). For example, a slow printer may be driven at 300 baud, a VDU at 4800 baud and an inter-computer link at 9600 baud.

There are two signal levels in common use:

(a) Voltage (V24), which uses logical 1 = −15 v to −3 V (normally −9V) and logical 0 = +3 V to +15 V (normally +9 V).

(b) Current (RS 232C), which uses logical 1 = 20 mA and logical 0 = 0 mA.

Notice that the quiescent line state is "active" in both cases (−9 V or 20 mA). This is particularly useful for fault finding because it indicates that at least the transmission circuit is made. The current loop uses optoisolation and consequently requires four wires for bi-directional communication in place of three wires for voltage (Tx, OV, Rx).

Before UARTs were introduced, the settings of baud rate, parity type and number of stop bits in transmit and receive devices were made by manual switch setting. Several UARTs allow these settings to be made by software, i.e. parallel output from computer to UART of a special code followed by this set-up information before transmission is attempted.

A block diagram of a microcomputer to VDU communication system is shown in Figure 4.14.

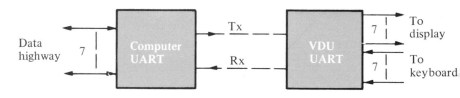

FIGURE 4.14 COMPUTER TO VDU SERIAL COMMUNICATION SYSTEM

Bi-directional serial communication can be:

(a) Duplex, i.e. transmission can occur in both directions at the same time—this is normal.

(b) Half-duplex, i.e. transmission can only occur in one direction at a time—one device must be "master" and the other "slave" in this system.

The pin connections on a 25-pin connector are shown in Table 4.1 (only the most important signals are included).

The last two signals are included to enable transmission to be made via a modem (this is described below). Request to Send is normally set permanently by the transmitting device but Clear to Send is the response from the receiving device and is used to stop transmission when the receiving device is busy. This is normally only used in the case of a printer when it requires the computer to stop transmitting whilst it prints previously transmitted text.

TABLE 4.1 RS 232C INTERFACE PIN CONNECTIONS

Pin No.	Function
1	Protective Ground
2	Transmit Data
3	Receive Data
4	Request to Send
5	Clear to Send
7	Signal Ground
8	Data Carrier Detect
20	Data Terminal Ready

For computer to VDU, or computer to computer communication which does not use a modem, it is normal to link pins 5, 8 and 20 to +9 V to make these signals permanently set.

Table 4.1 shows the signal connections for voltage signal levels (pins 2, 3 and 7). If 20 mA current loop is used spare pins, e.g. pin 14, 15, 16 and 17, can be utilised in place of pins 2, 3 and 7.

A modem is a device which is interposed between transmitting device and transmission line, and at the receive end of the circuit between transmission line and receiving device. It enables long-distance transmission to take place. The pattern of bits will often deteriorate due to pulse rounding for straightforward bit transmission. This effect is more pronounced at high baud rates. A modem modulates a carrier with the bit pattern, and the modulated sinewave is better able to survive long cable capacitive effects. A modem is not normally necessary for transmission distances below a few kilometres.

A final word of advice is offered as a result of the author's many frustrating commissioning exercises of long data links in a factory environment. Voltage signal level links do not perform as well as current loop links. The bit pulses do not deteriorate as badly with current loop, and data links can therefore be run at higher baud rates. Also current loop circuits tend to use optical isolation techniques so that important computer supplies are better protected from accidental short circuit on the transmission line/telephone cable.

Modem Frequencies (UK)
Tx "1" = 1180 Hz, Tx "0" = 980 Hz
Rx "1" = 1850 Hz, Rx "0" = 1650 Hz

Modem Frequencies (USA)
Tx "1" = 1270 Hz, Tx "0" = 1070 Hz
Rx "1" = 2225 Hz, Rx "0" = 2025 Hz

4.12 ANALOGUE/DIGITAL CONVERSION

The most important component in an analogue input system is the A/D (analogue/digital) converter. A/D converters can now be purchased on a single chip. The two most common techniques are:

4.12.1 Successive approximation method

In this technique the input voltage is compared with accurately known binary fractions of full scale.

Figure 4.15 shows the method of operation. The analogue voltage is balanced against a voltage which is derived from a reference voltage. This balancing process is one of successive approximation. The input voltage is firstly compared with half of the reference voltage (R only is switched into the circuit). If the input voltage is less than this reference, R is switched back out of circuit. Successively one-quarter, one-eighth, and so on, increments of the derived voltage are added to be compared with the input signal.

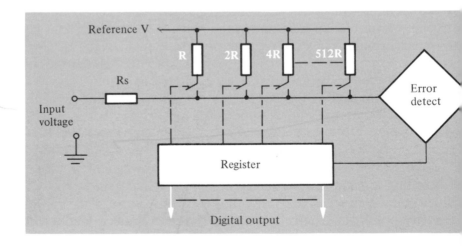

FIGURE 4.15 SUCCESSIVE APPROXIMATION A/D CONVERTER

For this 10-bit converter, 10 comparisons are made, until the final binary equivalent of the input voltage is read from the register.

Converters can be between 8-bit and 12-bit in length, with the latter type clearly offering the best resolution.

Successive approximation devices give good resolution at good speed—typically 20 μs conversion time. They are the most common A/D devices.

4.12.2 Integration method

This technique is commonly called the "double ramp" method and operates on the principle of counting pulses for a period which is proportional to the input voltage. Firstly, the input voltage is applied to an integrator circuit, as shown in Figure 4.16 (a) for a fixed time. Then a reference voltage of opposite polarity is switched to the integrator input, and the output ramps down at a fixed rate as shown in Figure 4.16 (b). During this downwards ramp a pulse stream is gated to a counter. Thus a large input voltage will cause a large voltage output of the integrator during the first half of the sequence, and this causes a large pulse count to occur in the second half.

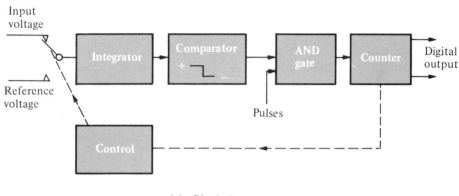

(a) Block diagram

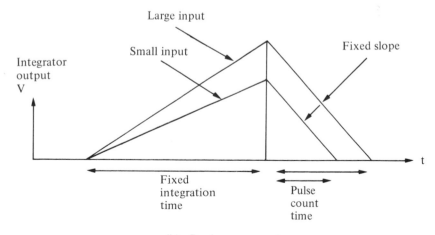

(b) Dual- ramp waveform

FIGURE 4.16 DUAL-RAMP INTEGRATION A/D CONVERTER

An integration A/D converter gives high resolution and can correct for drift but is slow—typically 50 msec or slower conversion time.

Notice that with any A/D converter which is slow in operation, it is advisable to stabilise the input signal using a "sample and hold" amplifier. This is simply an op-amp with a large capacitance across the input.

4.13 DIGITAL/ANALOGUE CONVERSION

A D/A converter is the heart of an analogue output system.

D/A converters are simpler than A/D converters. The almost universal method of operation is to use each bit of the digital version in order to generate different binary scaled voltages which are summed to produce the final analogue voltage.

The two methods of generating these binary multiples are:

4.13.1 Weighted-resistor D/A converter

The digital version (say 10 bits) is fed to a register, as shown in Figure 4.17. Each bit causes one resistor to switch a scaled value of a reference voltage to the analogue output line. For example, if the MSB (Most Significant Bit) is set to 1 then resistor $R/512$ will be switched in circuit. If the next bit is set to 1 then $R/256$ will switch in half of this voltage, and so on. Each resistor leg contributes a binary weighted voltage to the output.

The difficulty with this arrangement is that a large number of accurate but different resistor values is required.

Digital version

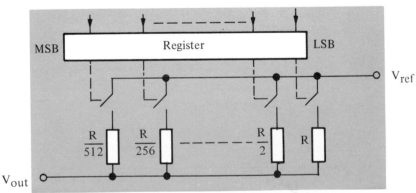

FIGURE 4.17 WEIGHTED-RESISTOR D/A CONVERTER

4.13.2 Resistor ladder D/A converter

This is the most common D/A converter. As Figure 4.18 shows, a similar technique is used. The ladder is constructed of resistors having only two values. There is no need to give a detailed description of circuit operation here—many textbooks on digital systems are available for that purpose.

However, it is worth while emphasising the difference between accuracy and resolution. Accuracy is determined by the precision of the resistor values in the resistor chain, and can vary between 0.05 to 0.1%. Resolution defines the smallest voltage increment that can be discerned, e.g. a 9-bit converter has a resolution of 1 part in 512, or 0.2%.

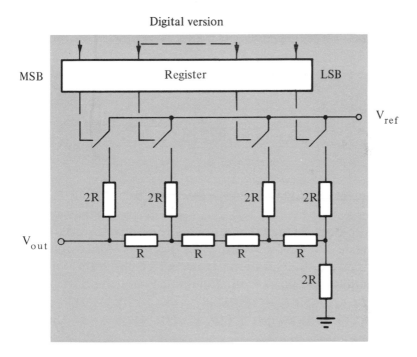

FIGURE 4.18 RESISTOR LADDER D/A CONVERTER

4.14 MULTIPLEXED INPUT/OUTPUT

If a microcomputer has a small plant interface it is conceivable to wire each analogue and digital input/output signal to a separate input/output channel. However, a large number of plant signals requires a large amount of input/output circuitry.

For example, 32 analogue inputs, for 10-bit A/D, requires 32 A/Ds and 320 digital input channels.

Plus 80 digital inputs, requires another 80 digital input channels, i.e. total of 400 digital input channels.

In this situation it is sensible to multiplex signals, i.e. allow them to share input/output channels.

A multiplexed analogue input system is shown in Figure 4.19. The system handles sixteen analogue inputs and a 4-bit channel address code is sent out (using 4 digital output lines) from the CPU. The multiplexer chip decodes this 4-bit address into sixteen discrete analogue channel-selection lines. Only one line will be selected so only that analogue input signal will be passed through to the A/D converter.

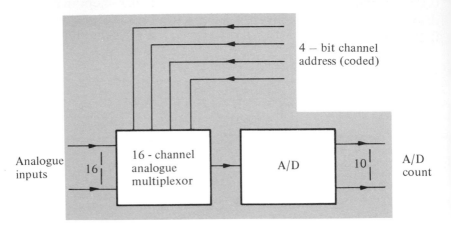

FIGURE 4.19 MULTIPLEXED ANALOGUE INPUT SYSTEM

Thus only fourteen digital input/output lines are required to handle sixteen analogue inputs. This is in place of sixteen A/D converters in a non-multiplexed configuration. However, a program which scans these channels must be written, and it must have the form:

OUTPUT CHANNEL ADDRESS

DELAY (TO ALLOW MULTIPLEXOR AND A/D TIME TO SETTLE)

READ A/D COUNT

DELAY

REPEAT FOR OTHER CHANNELS.

Digital input systems can also be multiplexed. Earlier we examined a multiplexed digital input system for scanning a keyboard. A plant interface of several dozen, or even several hundred, contact closure signals can be handled in the same way, as Figure 4.20 shows. In this case 4 digital output lines and 8 digital input lines handle $16 \times 8 = 128$ digital input contact closure signals. Note that the decoder chip enables the 4-bit address code to expand to strobe 1 of sixteen blocks of eight contact closures. The "blocking" diodes are to prevent the settings of unstrobed contacts affecting the strobed block of eight contacts.

Digital and analogue outputs can be multiplexed in the same way, but this is rarely done. The reason is that the security of outputs, which are often control signals, should be paramount. A circuit failure can cause one digital output to be sent out on the wrong plant interface line, e.g. a computer sending an indicator lamp signal could start a conveyor!

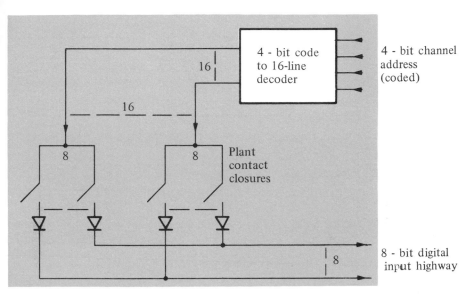

FIGURE 4.20 MULTIPLEXED DIGITAL INPUT SYSTEM

Similarly the benefits of multiplexing input signals may be overridden by the requirement for dedicated input circuitry. Remember that if a multiplexed A/D converter fails, all analogue inputs which use that converter will read incorrectly. Alternatively if one input/output chip fails (which is not unlikely when remote plant cabling is connected) in a multiplexed digital input/output, then all contact closures may be lost.

The choice of when to multiplex and when not to multiplex is a balance between price and system security, but beware of system manufacturers who hide or do not mention any multiplexing which they may perform.

4.15 SYSTEM BACK-UP (DUALITY)

In some applications it may be preferred to install back-up equipment to improve availability. The back-up may be:

(a) *Total back-up* of complete microcomputer system with the plant interface being scanned by two parallel systems. In this arrangement input contact closures will have to be duplicated so that both machines can scan the plant independently. Also digital and analogue outputs will have to be switched between machines with one machine acting as master and the other as standby. Automatic and manual switchover between machines are desirable in this configuration. This arrangement is shown in Figure 4.21. Any peripherals can also be duplicated.

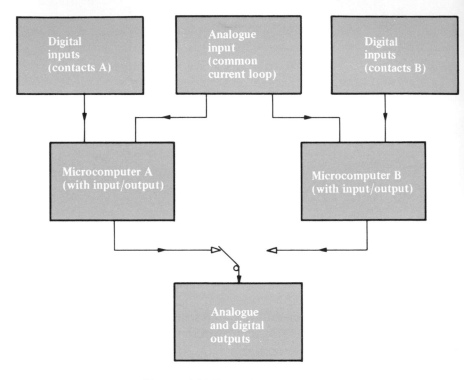

FIGURE 4.21 TOTAL SYSTEM BACK-UP

(b) *Partial back-up* in a system which involves a large plant interface which is mounted on separate boards from the CPU and memory. Figure 4.22 shows how the interface between input/output boards and CPU board can be switched between CPU boards. Such interface-switching systems are not uncommon with minicomputers and can be conveniently designed in LSI form for microcomputers. Of course the CPU and memory in a microcomputer represent a far more reliable module than for a minicomputer and the necessity for duplication of this type is more questionable.

(c) *Backing store back-up*. In an online system which employs a backing-store (floppy disc or hard disc) it is sensible to consider duplicating the drive and possibly also the control electronics. Clearly the electro-mechanical nature of the device makes it the most unreliable component.

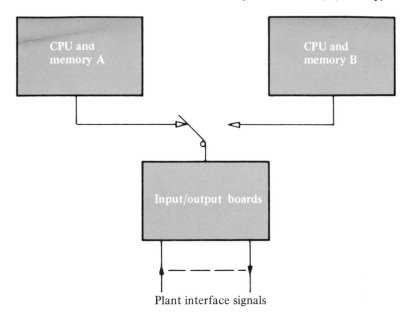

Plant interface signals

FIGURE 4.22 PARTIAL BACK-UP (CPU AND MEMORY)

A technique for detection of a computer-system failure is a "watch-dog", which can be applied in cases (a) and (b) above to trigger changeover from one machine to the other. A watchdog is a small hardware timing circuit which is driven by the computer software. Typically the timer circuit has an input/output address, and this address must be set at regular intervals, e.g. every 100 msec or faster otherwise a relay will become de-energised. This relay can be used for indication purposes, to sound an audible alarm or to trigger switch-over from one machine to another. Thus if the computer software fails to set this address regularly, perhaps due to a software "lock-up" or "crash", or if the machine is switched off or loses a power supply, the watchdog will trip.

FURTHER READING

1. Halsall, F. and Lister, P.F., *Microprocessor Fundamentals,* Pitman, London, 1980.
2. Artwick, B., *Microcomputer Interfacing,* Prentice-Hall, London, 1980.
3. Tocci, R. and Laskowiski, L.P., *Microprocessors and Microcomputers,* Prentice-Hall, London, 1979.

Chapter 5

VDU-based Systems for Plant Monitoring

5.1 MINIS AND MICROS FOR DISPLAY

In this section it will be difficult always to separate the minicomputer and the microcomputer because they often occur together in the same system. Thus a VDU-based monitoring system could consist of:

(a) a microcomputer alone (with VDU or TV monitor);
(b) a distributed processing system of microcomputers and minicomputers;
(c) the use of microcomputers for control functions (particularly 3-term controllers) and a minicomputer for display purposes.

The minicomputer is invariably a 16-bit machine but it is far more powerful than its 16-bit microcomputer counterpart for many reasons. It is faster and because it has been under commercial development for many years it has better supporting hardware modules (e.g. to perform multi-bit arithmetic, to buffer serial data from other computers) and software. Very powerful and flexible program organiser modules ("operating systems") enable minicomputers to handle large multi-programming systems. A typical minicomputer configuration can handle many peripherals, more than one backing store, several data links and even a large plant interface.

A recent development of minicomputers has been the introduction of microcomputers within their internal hardware system, e.g. to handle data-link handling. Undoubtedly this will intensify with new generations of minicomputers. Indeed minicomputers may become to look like distributed processing microcomputer systems.

One development of microcomputer technology into minicomputer design has been the introduction of the PDP LSI-11 minicomputer. The PDP 8 and 11 ranges of minicomputers (manufactured by the American firm DEC) have been by far the most successful, and the most recent model, the LSI-11, uses LSI construction techniques. This means that the machine is designed using microprocessors, ROM and RAM, but retains the computing power of the minicomputer.

Mention should be made of the leading range of British minicomputers—the Ferranti 500 (now superseded) and 700 series. Many of these machines are to be found in British chemical, oil and steel plants and in many other applications.

A final word should be said of the ubiquitous CRT. The CRT, in VDU or TV monitor form, is by far the most flexible and cheapest operator information device. When combined with a keyboard, its interactive use by a plant operator produces highly centralised data display and control facilities.

5.2 "SHARED DISPLAY" SYSTEMS

A "Shared Display" system is a concept of plant measurement monitoring, display and control which is based on a control panel or desk which contains nothing more than one, or a small number, of VDUs (normally colour). This is backed by electronic cubicles which provide transducer signal handling, controllers and display driving equipment (microcomputers and/or minicomputers). Printers and plant data-storage facilities (usually floppy disc) are normally included. The VDU-based control desk replaces the traditional large area (perhaps in more than one control room) of control panels and desks on which were mounted indicators, chart recorders, switches and control knobs. Operator interface is totally concentrated on the VDU.

Figure 5.1 shows a traditional control room. The author recalls a control room for a blast furnace which involved 90 square metres of steel panel to support all indicators, recorders, etc.!

Figure 5.2 shows the equivalent display and control facilities reduced to a VDU desk in a typical shared display system. The normal plant supervision requirements of data monitoring, alarm indication, trend recording and control-loop setpoint adjustment is performed via the VDU and keyboard.

All of the large instrument manufacturers now offer similar systems of this type, e.g. Kent (P4000 system), Taylor (MOD 111 system), Foxboro (FOX 111 system), Hartman and Braun (Contronic 3), Honeywell and others. In these systems minicomputer or microcomputer computing capability is linked via a parallel (sometimes serial) interface to VDUs, other peripherals, and instrumentation and control (3-term controllers) equipment.

Such systems have their application from small plants (perhaps several analogue and digital input signals, perhaps no controllers) up

FIGURE 5.1 CONTROL ROOM WITH QUICK-SCAN 1300 INSTRUMENTATION

FIGURE 5.2 MOD III

to complex chemical plant with several hundred plant input and out-put signals and even several hundred control loops. Note that to pre-serve system integrity (to maintain control in the event of equipment breakdown) discrete controllers (usually microprocessor-based) are provided for each control loop. These can be set manually if required.

Separate functions for particular applications, e.g. additional con-trol routines, perhaps utilising mathematical models, sequence or logic control, longer-term data storage, additional logging/plotting, etc., are normally handled in a separate but linked minicomputer or microcomputer.

Obviously an investment in a VDU-based system of this type becomes more effective for a large instrument-handling system.

5.3 TYPICAL PROPRIETARY "SHARED DISPLAY" SYSTEMS

5.3.1 Kent P4000 system

The Kent VDU-based display and control system is one of the latest of the shared display systems.

A generalised block diagram of the K90/P4000 system is shown in Figure 5.3.

A microcomputer-technology minicomputer, the PDP LSI 23, forms the heart of the system. It has up to 128 K of MOS memory and drives a floppy disc and several colour VDUs via the parallel DEC Q-Bus. Operator keyboards and an Engineer's keyboard operate over serial link. Banks of up to thirty-one controllers in each bank are interfaced. Each controller is itself microcomputer-based.

In the Plant Interface a plant input/output card can be of the following types:

(a) 16-channel analogue input;
(b) 4-channel analogue output;
(c) 32-channel steady digital input;
(d) 8-channel fleeting digital input (i.e. signal is staticised);
(e) 16-channel digital output;
(f) 4-channel pulse counting input;
(g) 8-channel incremental output.

This display system splits the plant into areas, and for each area several display formats are available—plant mimic with instrument readings superimposed numerically, trend recording (in place of chart recorders) and horizontal bar representation (in place of meters and indicators). The operator can make changes to controller setpoints using his keyboard.

The individual controllers are based on the 8-bit Motorola 6802 microprocessor and are linked to the Controller Interface by serial link. Their operation is described in Section 5.6.

Figure 5.4 shows the display formats which are available.

5.3.2 Other systems

The Foxboro FOX 3 system offers similar facilities but has less detailed mimic and trend display features. It concentrates on the ease of operator entry of control functions—continuous and batch. For example, Figure 5.5 shows a simple batch process and the program which the operator enters in the VDU to specify the computer's control role. The control task called CHARG involves the following steps:

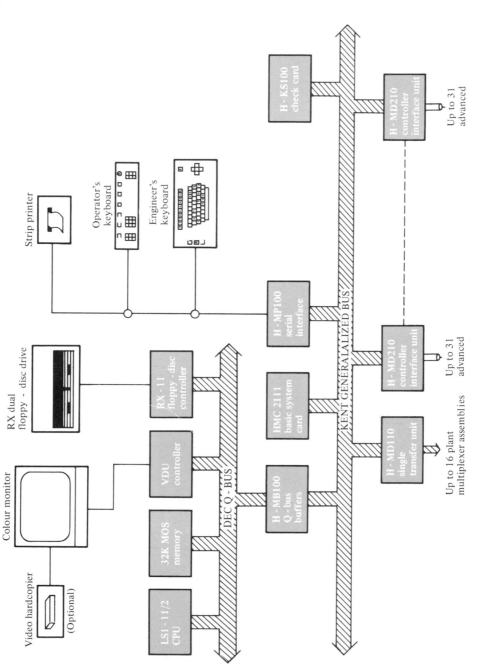

FIGURE 5.3 KENT K90/P4000 DISPLAY SYSTEM

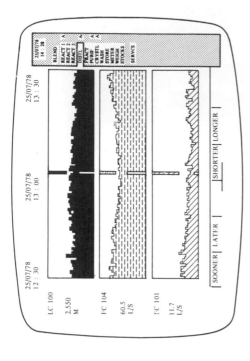

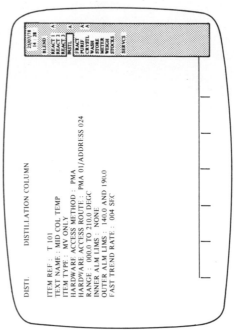

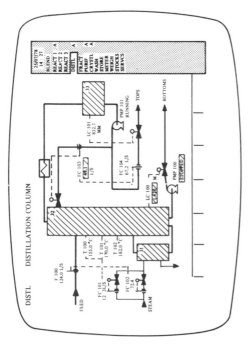

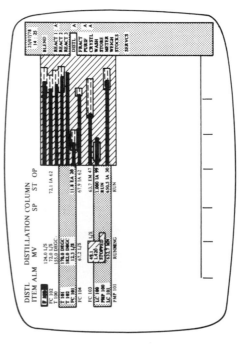

FIGURE 5.4 KENT P4000 DISPLAY FORMATS

(a) fill the tank to a level of 50% with material "A",

(b) fill the tank to a level of 75% with material 'B",

(c) start an agitator,

(d) heat the contents to 95°C,

(e) hold at that temperature for 20 minutes,

(f) stop the agitator,

(g) start the discharge pump,

(h) wait until the level is below 5%,

(i) stop the pump.

The specification (input/output address, signal range, etc.) of the plant signals are also specified by VDU entry using a different display format.

```
TASK CHARG
LET FILL A = ON
WAIT UNTIL LEVEL  > = 50.0
LET FILL A = OFF
LET FILL B = ON
WAIT UNTIL LEVEL  > = 75.0
LET FILL B = OFF
LET AGIT = ON
CALL SET ( TEMP,"SP", 95.0 )  ◄─────────── CALL SET means change the set point
WAIT UNTIL TEMP > 94.5
WAIT 1200  ◄────────────────── 1200 seconds = 20 minutes
CALL SET ( TEMP, "SP", 0.0 )
LET AGIT = OFF
LET PUMP = ON
WAIT UNTIL LEVEL  <5.0
LET PUMP = OFF
DEACT CHARG
END
```

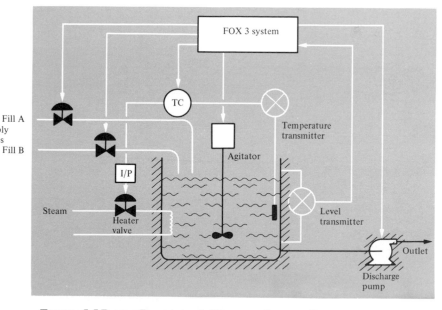

FIGURE 5.5 BATCH PROCESS AND FOXBORO PROCESS PROGRAM
(Courtesy Foxboro-Yoxall Limited)

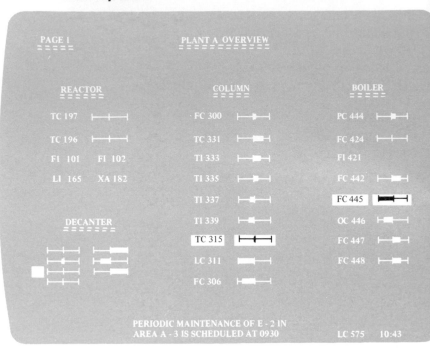

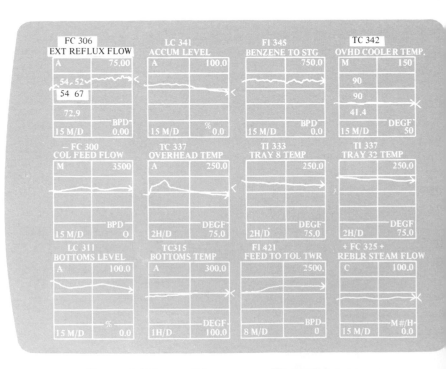

FIGURE 5.6 TAYLOR MONOCHROME TREND DISPLAY
(Courtesy Taylor Instrument Limited)

The heart of the system is the microprocessor-based FOX 3 Central Processor.

The Taylor MOD 111 system concentrates on monochrome (black and white) VDUs for much of its data display. Its controllers are again microprocessor-based. If the Taylor 1010 minicomputer is added colour displays of mimics and graphs are available.

Figure 5.6 shows the Taylor monochrome display of trends. Notice the high resolution of the graphs.

The range of equipment and facilities offered by other manufacturers is similar. The common theme is a strong dependence on the VDU or TV Monitor and an increasing use of microcomputers in various parts of these systems.

5.4 SMALL TAILORED DISPLAY SYSTEMS

The systems just described tend to be expensive and sometimes it is required to perform a single data logging and display function, i.e. for one plant area, on a small plant.

In this case a single microcomputer-driven VDU or TV monitor may well suffice. The display can be colour or monochrome. A small plant interface will be included.

Such a system will be tailored for the particular application. Plant data display can be a simple table of numerical information which is updated on a regular basis (e.g. every 5 seconds). Alternatively a detailed plant mimic may be drawn with plant readings added. The state of plant contacts and events can also be indicated by serial symbols or messages. Trend data can also be included.

A particular advantage of the use of a microcomputer plus memory mapped video (i.e. direct drive to a raster scan TV monitor) is that "full graphics" display facilities are available. This means that lines can be drawn from any point on the screen to any other. Thus detailed material flow and pipework can be drawn on a mimic or precise graphs can be drawn. The display design command to draw such a line is handled by software which inserts into the RAM screen data area the relevant bit combinations. This is not possible on a VDU which is driven by a standard serial link. Only the normal typewriter keyboard symbols are available. However, "semi-graphics" VDU controllers enable additional symbols to be used, and these can be designed to assist in the construction of realistically shaped plant vessels, valves, etc. The quality of displayed mimics and graphs is still not as good as DMA video drive direct from a microcomputer however.

5.5 MIMIC REPRESENTATION

(Firstly observe a copy of a typical colour VDU mimic in Figure 5.7. Note that this VDU format together with Figures 5.8, 5.9 and 5.10 are produced on a colour VDU computer system which has been developed by British Steel Corporation, Port Talbot Works, for a wide range of applications.)

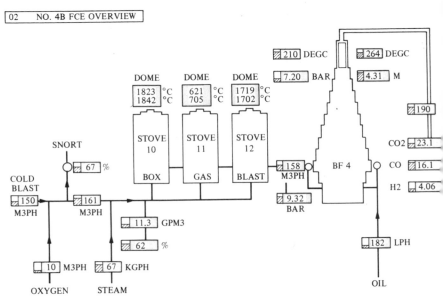

FIGURE 5.7 COLOUR VDU MIMIC OF PLANT

The art of designing a colour mimic of a plant area and superimposing dynamic data relating to instrument readings and other plant events/conditions is determined by factors such as:

(a) Select a sensible size for the plant area, e.g. the display should not be cluttered with over-detailed plant processing stages and pipework/material flow.

(b) It is tempting to over-use colour and to produce a dazzling but garish display. Clearly segregated processing stages need not always be coloured in different colours. It is useful to observe a colour code for pipework and material flows; a plant pipe painted-code may be in use, e.g. red for steam, blue for water, green for gas, orange for toxic gas, etc. This should be repeated on the mimic.

(c) Analogue readings, which may be instrument readings or possibly calculated values, can be superimposed on the mimic (the technique of doing this on a memory-mapped video drive is to use "shape tables"—this is described in Section 5.9). This numerical display information should not be updated more frequently than once every 5 seconds to prevent annoyance to the operator. Over-accurate representation of instrument readings, e.g. 47.315, may be sensible to the microcomputer but is unrealistic to an operator. The three most significant digits are normally satisfactory. It is sensible to add the engineering units, e.g. DEGC, BAR, LPM, etc., after numerical readings. Notice in Figure 5.7 how a small vertical bar, which is positioned just to the left of each numerical reading, represents the position of that instrument reading over its range. The colour of each block of numerical data could be altered, or the block could be flashed, when the instrument reading is in alarm, i.e. above or below alarm limits.

(d) Digital inputs representing plant or equipment states, e.g. pump on or off, valve open or closed, hopper discharge gate open or closed, etc., can control small areas of the display. In this way the colour of an isolating valve can alter when the valve changes from open to closed, or an arrow on the display can be added when a conveyor is switched into motion.

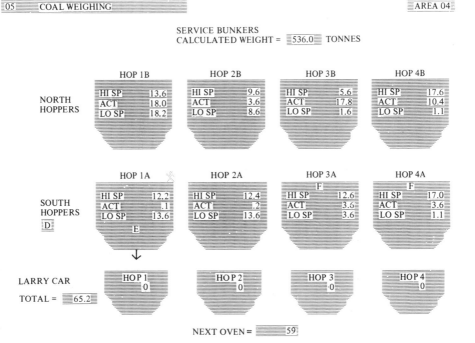

FIGURE 5.8 COLOUR VDU MIMIC OF BATCH PROCESS
(Courtesy British Steel Corporation, Port Talbot Works)

Whilst Figure 5.7 shows an updating mimic of a continuous process, a batch process can be represented in a similar manner as shown in Figure 5.8. In this application two sets of four weigh-hoppers can feed batches of different materials into a charging car. Analogue inputs feed the actual weights to the microcomputer/minicomputer, and digital inputs feed signals which indicate when the weigh-hoppers discharge (shown by an arrow for HOP 1A) and other events in the charging sequence. The computer can be controlling the sequence.

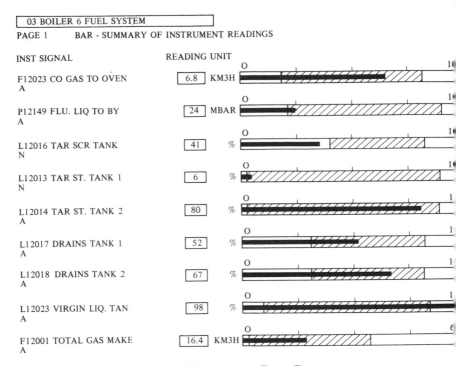

FIGURE 5.9 INSTRUMENT DATA DISPLAY

5.6 INSTRUMENT DATA DISPLAY

It is normally useful to concentrate the display of instrument readings and controller settings on to an additional separate format. This can include a bar representation of the reading (just like a strip indicator, e.g. car speedometer) and detailed information about the reading, e.g. range, units, alarm limits, input/output address. Figure 5.9 shows some of these features. The left-hand instrument reference, e.g. F12023, is the instrument loop number which is of value to the maintenance technician (note: F = flow). Several pages of this display may be necessary for a large number of signals. It would be possible for an operator to implement setpoint control using this display, e.g.

by keyboard entry of a new setpoint after positioning the cursor (a display position marker) at an appropriate position on the screen.

The background colour of the central portion of each "bar" can be chosen to be displayed in a different colour from the rest of the range. This will show the acceptable operating range of the instrument reading, i.e. if the reading is outside this range it is in alarm. If the reading is a controlled parameter (i.e. using a 3-term controller, possibly built into the microcomputer) the position of the setpoint can be marked in some way on the bar range.

Clearly many variations in the method of displaying numerical plant information are possible. However, it is worth emphasising the visual and ergonomic impact of the use of a coloured bar representation. The relative position of an instrument reading is clearly highlighted and this is often all that an operator requires.

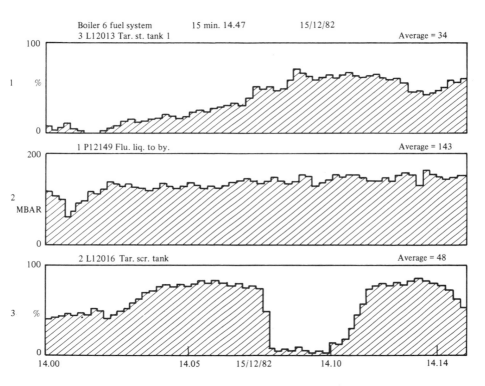

FIGURE 5.10 TREND (GRAPH) DISPLAY

5.7 TREND RECORDING

The bane of so many instrument mechanics is often the chart recorder. He spends much of his time unloading and storing rolls of chart paper (or even the old-fashioned circular chart), repairing faulty mechanical drives and clearing blocked-pen inking systems. VDU display of trends removes these chores and offers far greater flexibility in terms of selection of timescales and repositioning of the viewing time-window. All that is required is that the computer behind the VDU/TV monitor has sufficient memory to store the required plant data.

There are two basic methods of drawing graphical plots of historical plant data. One is to draw lines between each print which is to be plotted. The other is to "fill in" the graph by simply drawing coloured columns up to the required level for each point plotted, i.e. in the manner of a histogram. It is the author's contention that the latter produces far clearer and more readable displays. Messrs. Kent agree and Messrs. Taylor Instruments do not!

Figure 5.10 shows such a display. Each column represents an averaged value for that period. For example, if the analogue inputs are scanned every 5 seconds, and a 60-column graph represents 1 hour, then each 1-minute column is an average of 12 scanned readings. Of course it is unlikely that main memory can store these readings and so a floppy disc (occasionally magnetic tape cassette) is used for this purpose.

If too many instrument trends are crammed onto a single screen format, the display will look cluttered and graph resolution will be lost. Three graphs per display is common, and this coincides with the familiar 3-pen chart recorder.

The ability of the operator to change the timescale is useful; this can be initiated by operation of a pushbutton or keyboard key. Perhaps the last 15 minutes, 1 hour, 8 hours (shift) or even 24 hours (in the case of a slow process) can be displayed. Stored readings for these extended timescales will obviously be condensed, i.e. the 8 hours graph will use 8-minute averages.

In some systems the time window can be moved, i.e. after a particular timescale has been selected—say 1 hour—that 1 hour of historical data can be shifted back to the previous hour, and so on.

It is sometimes required to obtain a hard copy of a trend display. This is best achieved using a video copier which takes the VDU video signal and converts it (in monochrome) to a photocopy of the screen format.

5.8 ONLINE DESIGN FACILITIES

In a small microprocessor-based display application it would not normally be required to alter display formats or to change the signal list. In a larger system it is often a requirement to be able to extend or alter the signal lists, change mimic layouts or re-group instruments which are graphed on the same trend display. Clearly it would be inconvenient to take such a system offline in order to load new data and display specification files.

Several systems include online facilities to reformat and even create new display formats, particularly for mimic displays. A trained operator can then draw and colour a plant mimic and specify the screen positions and identities of dynamic data representation. Additionally signal lists can be altered and extended using the VDU keyboard. This is particularly useful if an instrument reading is re-ranged or alarm limits are adjusted.

5.9 PRINTER LOGGING

In a small display or control application no printer logs may be required. However, sometimes it is required to produce printed logs of the following type:

5.9.1 Alarm logs

Typically one line of a standard format is printed whenever a plant instrument reading goes into alarm, e.g.

Time	Instrument Reference	TEMP AMMONIA EXHAUSTER HIGH Instrument Text (if stored)	Current Reading	Alarm Level
16.23	T1849	EXHAUSTER HIGH	369	DEGC (350)

5.9.2 Event logs

Event logs are particularly related to digital inputs and provide a record of when significant plant events occur, e.g. in a charging sequence, controller mode change, valve operation, etc. An example line could be:

09.48 HOPPER 3 GATE OPEN

5.9.3 Production logs

A production log represents a summary of plant operations perhaps over a period of a shift or a day. Average values of plant readings, typically 1-hour averages, are normally required. Operations managers often like to see:

(a) Hourly averages.
(b) Spot readings at end of each hour or shift, e.g. for vessel levels.
(c) Maximum and minimum readings.
(d) Totals, e.g. total flow or total weight.

5.9.4 Technical log

A separate log is sometimes required to summarise technical operating parameters. These are usually calculations which are performed on plant measurements, e.g.

(a) Plant efficiency.
(b) Gas utilisation.
(c) Required burden.
(d) Product analysis, etc.

FURTHER READING

Information on the many different computer display systems is not documented in other textbooks. The reader is referred to handbooks which manufacturers publish to advertise and support their systems.

Chapter 6

Modes of Control

6.1 GENERAL METHODS OF COMPUTER CONTROL

A computer can assist plant control in two different manners:

(a) Continuous control, i.e. the computer generates an analogue control signal.
(b) On/off control, i.e. the computer switches a remote piece of equipment or provides a sequence of on/off signals in a batch process.

In a continuous control system the computer can continuously regulate a plant parameter either:

(i) directly—called "direct" control;
(ii) by supplying a required setting to an external controller—called "supervisory" control;
(iii) via an operator, who may or may not implement the computer's recommended change—called "advisory" control.

Sections 6,2 to 6.6 describe principles of continuous control.

"On-off" control which is used in a batch process is described in Sections 6.7 and 6.8.

Finally Section 6.9 describes methods of modelling a process mathematically to assist in setting up the plant correctly and also to assist control during actual plant operation. Section 6.10 summarises more complex control strategies.

One microcomputer control application which was briefly described in section 1.4.4 is Numerical Control. This technique is highly specialised and was briefly described as providing a sequence of position settings for a milling machine. This application will not be discussed in more detail here.

125

6.2 PRINCIPLE OF CONTINUOUS CONTROL

It is perhaps worth while to summarise here the main principles of classical control analysis.

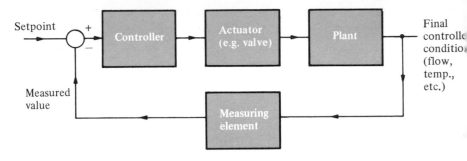

FIGURE 6.1 GENERALISED CONTROL LOOP

Figure 6.1 shows a generalised block diagram of a control loop which regulates plant flow, pressure, temperature, level, etc. A feedback signal, which is a measurement of the plant parameter which is being controlled, is compared with (i.e. subtracted from) the setpoint. Any deviation is applied to the controller. The controller processes this signal in a variety of ways before applying a correction signal to the actuator, which is normally a valve. The plant is the heating vessel, rolling mill, chemical process, gas supply unit, or whatever other process is being controlled.

The controller has traditionally been a pneumatic, electronic or even hydraulic box of gadgetry which can be set by technicians/engineers to regulate the plant in a particular way.

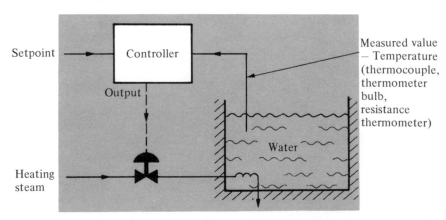

FIGURE 6.2 TEMPERATURE CONTROL LOOP

Figure 6.2 shows a typical temperature-control loop. If the controller output to the valve is proportional to the input deviation (i.e. Setpoint—Measured Value), the controller is said to be a PROPORTIONAL controller.

The PROPORTIONAL BAND is said to be 100% if (for a constant Setpoint) the percentage change in valve movement equals the percentage change in measured value. However, if the valve movement is twice that of the measured value the Proportional Band is 50%.

Example

If the temperature range of the measured value is 0–100°C,
Valve fully closed gives 30°C,
and
Valve fully open gives 70°C,
then

$$\text{Proportional Band} = \frac{70-30}{100-0} \times 100\% = 40\%$$

Thus the lower the Proportional Band, the higher is the GAIN of the controller.

Unfortunately a simple proportional controller rarely produces adequate control. The main difficulty is a phenomenon called OFFSET. Offset occurs due to a load change.

Consider the water temperature-control system just described and assume that the valve has forty divisions of movement. If the valve is twenty divisions open, temperature is 50°C. Let us assume that the water temperature starts at 48°C and this causes the valve to open by two divisions. This will cause more heating steam to flow, which will drive the temperature up to 50°C to correct for the error. However, if an additional cold-water load is subsequently added to the tank, the temperature may fall again by 2°C. The valve will open by two divisions but this time the temperature will not rise because the additional steam is used to heat the additional water and not raise the temperature of the original load. Thus the additional load has caused an error or OFFSET. Proportional control cannot correct for this load change on its own and INTEGRAL control must be added.

Integral Control adds a correction term which increases the longer the deviation (or error) persists. Thus it integrates the deviation. Figure 6.3 illustrates these effects for a Proportional Plus Integral Controller. In response to a step change in input deviation, the controller produces a step-output component plus a steady ramp component in the opposite direction.

Mathematically this is expressed:

Output $= -K_1\theta - K_2\int\theta.\ \mathrm{d}t$

where $\theta =$ deviation (or error).

K_1 and K_2 are gain factors for proportional and integral control respectively.

The integral term indicates a time sum of the error.

A Proportional+Integral controller will therefore remove offset and produce good control.

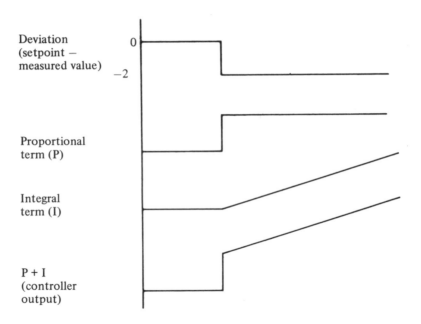

FIGURE 6.3 STEP RESPONSE OF A PROPORTIONAL+INTEGRAL CONTROLLER

A third term is often added to a controller to give DERIVATIVE control. This applies a correction term which is related to the rate of change of deviation. Figure 6.4 shows the response of a derivative term to a typical input-deviation characteristic which ramps down, stabilises for a short period and then ramps up again. The derivative term consists of two "pulses":

(a) The first "pulse" operates in the same direction as proportional and integral control, and thus assists these control terms. This is particularly useful when a large change occurs in the measured value.

(b) The second "pulse" operates in the opposite direction to proportional and integral control. This helps to prevent overshoot and instability in the control loop.

Derivative control is never applied on its own. In fact most controllers offer the three terms. Thus the mathematical expression for a 3-term controller is:

$$\text{Output} = \frac{-100}{\text{PB}} \left(\theta + \frac{1}{\text{IAT}} \int \theta . dt + \text{DAT} . \frac{d\theta}{dt} \right)$$

where PB = Proportional Band (inverse of proportional gain),
     IAT = Integral Action Time (inverse of integral gain),
     DAT = Derivative Action Time (derivative gain).

The technique of adjusting the three control knobs on the front of a controller (PB, IAT and DAT) to optimise control loop operation is called "tuning" the controller.

Typical controller settings for a slow temperature-control loop may be:
    PB   = 30%,
    IAT = 30 minutes,
    DAT = 10 minutes.

The settings for a fast flow-control loop may be:
    PB   = 150%,
    IAT = 0.5 minute,
    DAT = 0 minute.

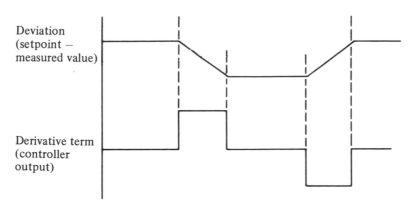

FIGURE 6.4 RESPONSE OF A DERIVATIVE CONTROLLER

6.3 CONVENTIONAL CONTROLLERS

6.3.1 Pneumatic controller

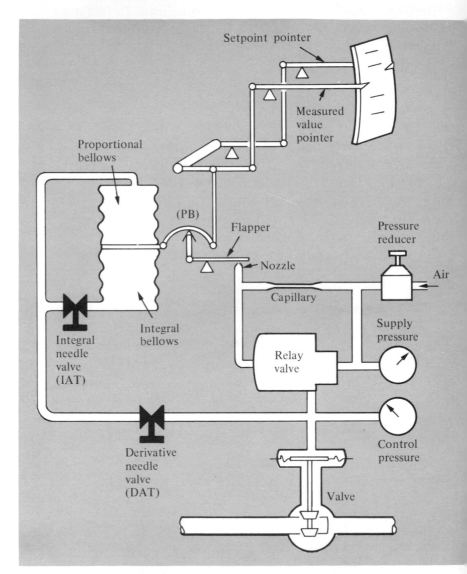

FIGURE 6.5 PNEUMATIC CONTROLLER

A practical 3-term pneumatic controller is shown in Figure 6.5. The position of the Setpoint Pointer is normally set manually. The position of the Measured Value Pointer is controlled by a signal from the measuring instrument, e.g. pressure from bourdon tube. The difference between these two positions is the Deviation (or error) and this difference is passed through the mechanical lever system to move a flapper. The position of this flapper which is adjacent to a fixed nozzle determines the air pressure in the nozzle. Thus a positive deviation causes a build-up in pressure in the nozzle. This pressure is amplified in the relay valve and applied to the diaphragm of a regulating valve.

An internal feedback system operates from this output pressure to dampen flapper movement to achieve the three control terms (PB, IAT and DAT). A proportional bellows together with a curved lever generate the proportional term, with the position of the pointed lever on the curved lever determining the PB. An integral bellows and integral needle valve provide a variable integral term, with the adjustment of the needle valve providing the setting of the IAT. An additional derivative needle valve provides the derivative term; the DAT is given by the setting of this valve.

The pneumatic controller has dominated industrial control applications for a long period but it has been challenged by the electronic controller and very recently by the microprocessor controller.

6.3.2 Electronic controller

The heart of an electronic controller is an Op-amp as described in section 3.14. This simple circuit (now in single-chip form) can provide subtraction between Setpoint and Measured Value AND generate the three control terms AND sum these terms. A simplified representation of this circuit is shown in Figure 6.6. The summing amplifier feature of the Op-amp can provide subtraction between Setpoint and Measured Value (if Measured Value is firstly inverted) to produce a Deviation signal. The three potentiometers enable the three controller settings to be adjusted.

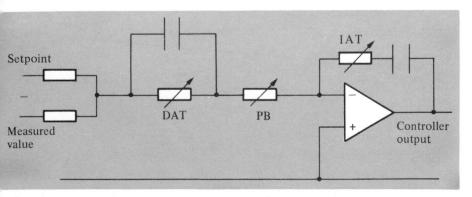

FIGURE 6.6 ELECTRONIC CONTROLLER (SIMPLIFIED CIRCUIT)

6.4 SUPERVISORY CONTROL

Supervisory Control is the technique of using a computer to provide the setpoint to a controller. A typical system may have several setpoints to individual controllers.

The particular advantage of this control technique is that the computer can choose the desired values for several plant parameters, but the autonomous controllers ensure loop security in the event of computer failure.

Controllers which are used in this mode generally have the switching options shown in Figure 6.7. A changeover switch on the front of the controller selects a setpoint either from the normal internal setpoint knob or from a remote device. This is normally a computer, but could be the output of another controller which is connected in "cascade" mode. The computer's setpoint is normally in one of the preferred signal ranges, e.g. 0–10 V. An additional feature which many controllers possess is a changeover switch on the signal connection to the Regulating Unit (valve). This enables the normal controller output signal connection to be broken and a manual adjustment to be made directly to the valve. This is helpful if the controller itself malfunctions. This signal injection point can also be used if the computer performs the controller's function and generates the 3-term control signal itself. The controller can then be used as a standby device.

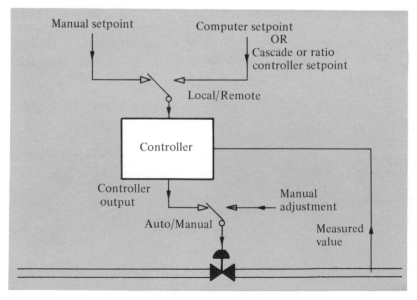

FIGURE 6.7 SUPERVISORY CONTROL — CONTROLLER SWITCHING OPTIONS

A desirable feature of a supervisory control system is "bumpless" changeover in the event of a controller changing from computer to manual setpoint. The manual setpoint should be set to the same value as the computer setpoint to prevent a step change in the control loop when switchover occurs. This can be achieved in two ways:

(a) The computer should display (probably on a VDU) its setpoint so that an operator can adjust the manual setpoint to this value before changeover.

(b) The manual setpoint should automatically track the computer setpoint. This is particularly desirable if automatic changeover occurs, e.g. the changeover switch is activated by the computer (probably using its watchdog) when it fails.

One method of effecting manual setpoint tracking is to use the computer setpoint to physically drive (using a servo or a stepper motor) the manual setpoint dial.

A disadvantage of applying an analogue output signal as a controller setpoint is that if the circuit is lost due to a circuit fault, wiring disconnection, power supply failure, etc., the setpoint will immediately collapse to zero. Thus one or more control valves may be fully closed in a fault situation.

A better method is to use an incremental output, which will leave the setpoint at the last value when such a fault occurs. This can be performed using Raise/Lower pulses (2 digital outputs) from the computer, as shown in Figure 6.8. The pulses can be used to drive a stepper motor (within the controller) which positions a setpoint

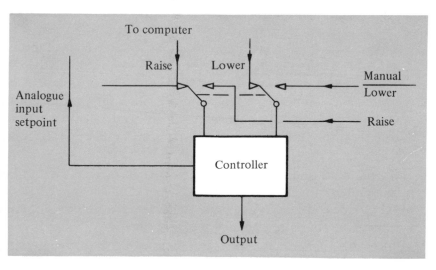

FIGURE 6.8 INCREMENTAL SUPERVISORY CONTROL

potentiometer. The standby manual setpoint can also be adjusted by a Raise/Lower system (two pushbuttons) in this arrangement. A feedback signal (analogue input) is necessary from the controller to the computer so that the computer knows exactly the value of the setpoint.

In supervisory control it is sometimes necessary for the controller to have a special feature of not using proportional control, and more frequently derivative control, to prevent loop instability (prolonged instability) for setpoint changes.

6.5 DIRECT DIGITAL CONTROL (DDC)

In Direct Digital Control (DDC) the computer operates as the 3-term controller, and it controls plant regulators (valves, pumps, heaters, etc.) directly.

DDC using minicomputers was heralded as a major transformation in plant-control strategy in the late 1960s. However, after many applications the concept has become largely discredited for one major reason. Relying on one machine for complete control of a plant introduces a dangerous dependence on a single piece of equipment. If the machine is backed up with a complete set of discrete controllers the cost increases enormously and one wonders what is the purpose of the computer at all. Even if a second standby computer is used, the security of the changeover system and the autonomy (e.g. do the computers share the same electrical supply, the same air-conditioning plant, etc.?) of the two machines gives cause for concern. Having said this several DDC systems do exist, particularly in oil refineries and large chemical plants which possess hundreds of control loops.

A computer program generates and sums the three control terms. The controller settings—PB, IAT and DAT—can normally be adjusted by manual entry via a VDU or keyboard. The setpoint can be entered into the computer by the operator, although in some more complex control systems the computer will generate its own setpoint.

The method of control signal output to the regulator can be of several types:

(a) Continuous analogue signal (e.g. 4 to 20 mA). This can be generated by a D/A converter.

(b) The same continuous analogue signal but generated using two digital output pulse signals from the computer.

The pulses are applied to a simple integrator circuit (Op-amp with capacitor feedback) to generate the analogue signal which drives the valve. Alternatively the analogue memory can take the form of a

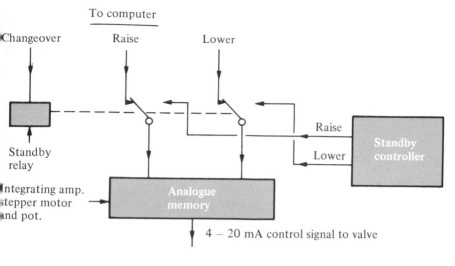

FIGURE 6.9 DDC INCREMENTAL OUTPUT

stepper motor which drives a potentiometer or even a servo follower. Such a system is shown in Figure 6.9. This type of incremental output is called BOUNDLESS and has the advantage of providing a continuous control signal to the regulator when the computer output fails. Also it can give bumpless transfer to a standby controller if the standby controller also has incremental output.

(c) An incremental output (raise/lower pulses) driving an *incremental* valve (rather than a valve which requires a continuous analogue position signal). Such a system involves a stepper motor driving the valve directly.

The most common valve regulator is the pneumatic diaphragm type, which requires a continuous analogue control signal. Electrical activators tend to be more expensive and unreliable. Thus an E/P (electric/pneumatic) converter is often required. A typical construction consists of a synchronous or stepper motor driving a cam which tensions a spring. The spring controls, perhaps using a bellows, the pneumatic output of the converter.

Minicomputer DDC systems can be duplicated at lower cost in microcomputers. However, the very low cost of the microcomputer has pushed its application more towards the microcomputer-based controller, as described next.

6.6 MICROCOMPUTER 3-TERM CONTROLLER

Several manufacturers have introduced controllers which are based on microcomputers. They tend to be cheaper and far more flexible than their predecessors.

A typical microcomputer controller is shown in Figure 6.10. It is based on the 8-bit Motorola 6802 microprocessor and has ROM and battery-backed RAM (in case of temporary loss of power). It provides one-, two- or three-term control and characterisation of setpoint and measured value signals. The characterisation functions can be selected from ratio with bias, root extraction and third-order polynomial. The output can be analogue or incremental. Provision is made for connections to a portable VDU and to a remote computer by serial link. The remote computer can load downline the controller settings (PB, IAT, DAT) and read back the setpoint, measured value and other data for display purposes.

Manual adjustment of PB, IAT and DAT is not performed in the usual manner of turning knobs. An engineer's panel and 8-digit digital display are used instead. The RAM locations which hold these settings can be examined and updated using this panel.

Thus the microcomputer controller represents an ideal application for a microprocessor and will undoubtedly dominate the 3-term controller market in the future.

6.7 ON/OFF AND BATCH CONTROL

Very little requires to be said about on/off control. It is so simple!

The computer simply sends out digital output signals to remote equipment to perform a variety of switching functions, such as:

(a) Switching on and off motors, pumps, isolating valves, conveyors, vibrating screens, hopper gates, charging cars, heaters etc.

(b) Supplying a parallel interface for a required weight, position etc., e.g. 4×4 BCD (16 lines total) for demanded weight to a remote weighing system.

A simple microcomputer with only one or two input/output chips can handle a small sequence-control system. Such a system could replace a conventional contactor and relay panel in the control of charging weigh-feeders, conveyors and charging skip in a particular sequence. Logic operations can be easily incorporated, e.g. do not run conveyor if skip is not in charging position, do not operate more than one weigh-feeder at any time, etc. Time delays can be readily included. Some systems, e.g. the PLC (programmable logic controller), which was briefly described in Section 1.4, may possess keyboard and display (small VDU) facilities to re-specify the logic sequence if necessary.

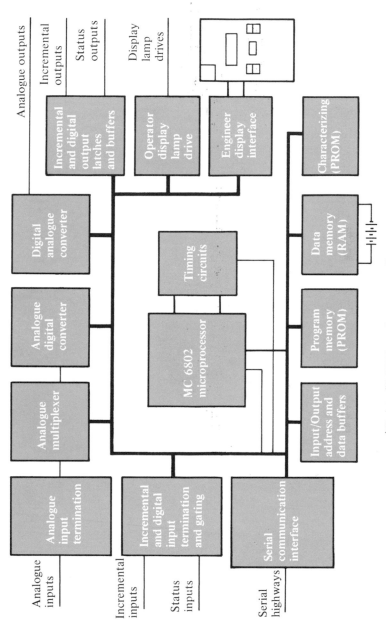

FIGURE 6.10 KENT ADVANCED CONTROLLER

All of these functions are, of course, operated through the plant interface using software which produces the output control signals in a correct logical sequence and with the required delays. Thus the control program is designed, possibly flow-charted, written and tested only after a careful analysis of sequence operation. A software simulation of the actual plant operation is often useful to fully test the control program.

An on/off control system of this type can include analogue inputs, e.g. a weight or temperature signal, which may be limit checked to determine if a switched output signal must be set.

An alternative approach to remote switching is the use of a computer-to-computer data link for the transmission of switching signals. A serial link may be required for data collection and this can be used to give centralised switching-control facilities without the need to install extra cabling to handle several discrete signals. Thus in place of a bank of centrally located on/off and start/stop signals cabled directly to remote equipment, an operator can use a VDU and keyboard to select a switching operation. A message is transmitted serially to a remote data-collection microcomputer and the switching signal can be generated as a contact closure to control the necessary equipment. This arrangement is shown in Figure 6.11.

Obviously this technique can be expanded to include transmission of demanded weights, etc., to remote data-collection microcomputers which may be used for dedicated weighing system control.

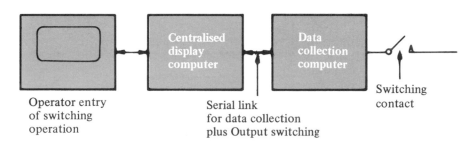

Operator entry of switching operation

Serial link for data collection plus Output switching

Switching contact

FIGURE 6.11 OUTPUT SWITCHING USING SERIAL LINK

6.8 MATHEMATICAL MODELLING

More powerful microcomputers can mimic those minicomputers which include programs which model the plant. These models are used to produce advisory control to operators, usually by way of VDU displays, in order to set up the process correctly or to modify plant settings on a continuous basis. Of course control advice can be implemented directly.

Plant modelling can be categorised into the following two types.

6.8.1 Static models

Static models are really only a series of calculations. They are often only run once before a batch process starts up. Alternatively they are run whenever a continuous process is to be altered in some way.

They are most commonly chargeweight models, although required settings for fuel flows may also be advised.

A typical static or chargeweight model balances the materials (both solids and fuel gases) which are available against the required product mix and generates a recommended burden and recommended gas flow rates. The model therefore is essentially a set of chemical and mass balancing equations. Thus it normally requires to know the chemical and sometimes physical analyses of the materials involved.

Table 6.1 lists the principal inputs and outputs of a static model for an iron blast furnace.

TABLE 6.1 STATIC MODEL FOR AN IRON BLAST FURNACE

Inputs
1. Analyses of iron ores available
2. Analysis of coke
3. Analyses of fluxes available
4. Required iron analysis
5. Required iron temperature

Outputs
1. Batch weight or iron ores
2. Batch weight of coke
3. Batch weight of fluxes
4. Blast volume (blowing rate)
5. Blast temperature

Analysis information for the materials involved could be entered manually via a VDU or perhaps automatically from computer-controlled analysers.

The operator runs the model using his VDU whenever a burden change is necessary, i.e. when material availability changes, or whenever a new analysis is available.

6.8.2 Dynamic models

A dynamic model is a plant simulation which is used in a feedback mode. Actual plant measurements—instrument reading and weights of charged materials—are fed in to the model which is run on a repetitive basis. This may be every few minutes or even less frequently for a slow process. The series of calculations in the model attempt to repeat the heat and mass (or chemical) changes which are occurring in the plant. If the model predicts that the final product will be off specification it produces recommended changes which should correct for such discrepancies.

An example of the use of a dynamic model is in the control of a BOS (Basic Oxygen Steelmaking) plant. Figure 6.12 shows the plant arrangement and the model inputs and outputs. A burden of molten iron, scrap and fluxes is charged to the vessel and an oxygen lance is lowered to a position just above the burden surface. Oxygen at a variable rate is blown for approximately 20 minutes with an adjustable lance height.

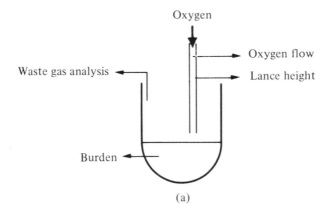

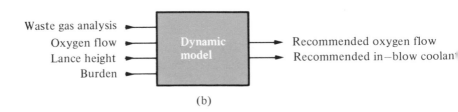

FIGURE 6.12 DYNAMIC MODEL OF BOS STEELPLANT

The model is fed with all of these readings. The burden may consist of at least six weights. Additionally the most important set of readings relating to waste-gas analysis (three readings) is also fed to the model. Effectively the waste-gas analysis is an indication of how the plant is operating compared with how it may have been expected to operate.

The dynamic model uses heat and mass balance equations, or it can be based on totally empirical relationships, to predict:

(a) final product analysis and temperature if current operation conditions are unaltered;
(b) change to oxygen flow to obtain target analysis and amount of coolant to be added if final temperature is too high.

Obviously the specification of both dynamic and static model programs requires detailed chemical knowledge of the processes involved. Additionally such models generally have to be tuned to the particular application.

6.9 MORE COMPLEX CONTROL TECHNIQUES

6.9.1 Cascade control

Cascade control is the technique of using the output of one controller as the setpoint of another. Thus two controllers are used with only one regulator.

Figure 6.13 shows the method of connection. The reason for the

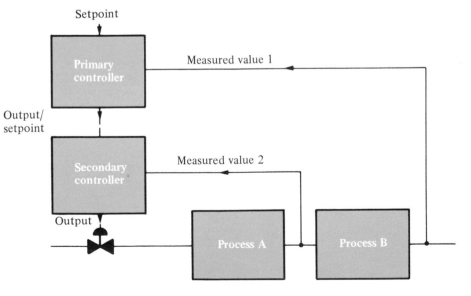

FIGURE 6.13 CASCADE CONTROL

application of cascade control is that it helps to remove the effect of large disturbances which may occur near the regulating unit (the valve).

If supervisory control or DDC is being applied then the control programs must have some form of linking mechanism so that the output of one algorithm (control routine) can feed into another to cater for cascade control.

6.9.2 Adaptive control

The use of a dynamic model, which was described above, is one type of adaptive control.

Adaptive control is the technique of assessing plant performance and adapting the control strategy to maximise the result.

An example is the measurement of product quality, e.g. analysis of a final plant mix, and the calculation of perhaps the mean squares of deviation from desired analysis. This error signal is then used to alter the gain of a control loop (or the setpoint) or the ratio by which a certain constituent is added.

6.9.3 Optimal control

Optimal control is the technique of designing a plant control system to achieve an optimum performance. Because it is concerned with design and is heavily dependent on modern mathematical control theory, it is not normally relevant to computer application in the field.

FURTHER READING
1. Jones, E.B., *Instrument Technology,* Vol. 3 (Telemetering and Automatic Control), Butterworth, London, 1975.
2. Yousefzadeh, B., *Basic Control Engineering,* Pitman, London, 1979.
3. Young, R.E., *Supervisory Remote Control Systems,* Peter Peregrinus Ltd., Stevenage, 1977.

Chapter 7

Microcomputer System Software

7.1 PROGRAMMING TECHNIQUES

In Section 2.12 the main concepts of program flow were discussed. These involve the normal sequential operation of program instructions which can be broken for the operation of:

   (a) loops,
   (b) subroutines,
and (c) interrupts.

When a program requirement is specified the design of the program solution is often called an "algorithm". An algorithm is the statement of the problem and the step-by-step solution.

It is often useful, especially in the case of inexperienced programmers, to draw a "flow-chart" for the program solution before actually attempting to write the program.

Example. State the algorithm and draw the flow chart of a simple program to display the quantity and price of petrol dispensed from a petrol pump.

ALGORITHM. The program reads a digital flowmeter which indicates petrol flow and a "star" rating switch. When the flow changes the program updates a display of quantity and price of petrol dispensed.

Notice the standard shapes which are used to represent the following actions:

   (a) Oval shape = terminator in program (start and end).
   (b) Rectangular shape = normal processing activity.
   (c) Diamond shape = decision.

The programmer can then use the algorithm description and the flow chart to code up his program.

143

FLOW CHART:

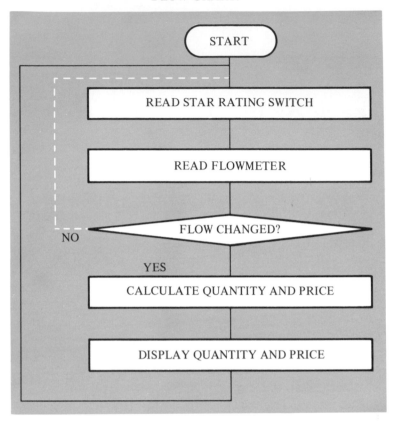

When designing a complex program it is sensible to follow an orderly sequence, as follows:
   (i) Define the problem.
  (ii) Design the solution—partition into functional blocks.
 (iii) Flowchart the program blocks.
  (iv) Write the program blocks.
   (v) Test and debug each block.
  (vi) Test and debug the entire program.
Fragmenting the program into sections in this manner allows the program to be tested in small pieces which makes it much easier to find errors.

The technique of "structured programming" is commonly applied. Many competent programmers will use this approach in any case, without being aware of the terminology and theory of the technique. In structured programming the overall program organisation is planned, perhaps with the aid of an overall flowchart. Then individual flowcharts can be prepared for each program module as it is designed, tested and corrected in turn. Each module should be fairly autonomous in operation with a single input and output.

7.2 PROGRAMMING LANGUAGES

There are three levels of programming language—machine code, assembly and high level.

MACHINE CODE is the binary code which is stored in memory ROM or RAM for each program instruction.

ASSEMBLY LANGUAGE is a representation of machine code using mnemonics for the instruction operator (e.g. ADD for adding a register to the accumulator) and labels for memory addresses (e.g. JMP SEND, where SEND refers to the address of another instruction). Thus it has a 1:1 correspondence with machine code, but makes the programmer's job much easier. He does not have to work out binary or hexadecimal codes for each program instruction.

HIGH-LEVEL LANGUAGES allow the programmer to use statements which are similar to spoken language. Such a statement can then be converted by a high-level language COMPILER program into perhaps several machine code instructions. Whilst a programmer needs to know details of the hardware of the microprocessor when writing in machine code or assembler, he can write high-level language programs which can run on many types of machines.

Programs which are written in a high-level language tend to use more memory than machine code or assembler programs, but it is far easier and quicker to program in a high-level language. However, a large compiler program is required to convert a high-level language "source" program to machine code ("object code").

An assembler program which converts from assembly language to machine code is smaller and is often held as firmware, i.e. in ROM.

Example. Consider the implementation of a simple add operation in the three programming languages for a 16-bit microprocessor.

High-level language
    X = Y + Z
i.e. one line of programming.

Assembly language:
LOAD Y Load Accumulator with Number in Memory Address Y
ADD   Z Add Number in Memory Address Z
STO   X Store Answer in X

Machine code (in Hexadecimal):

03C4 0100	LOAD Y
2A05 0101	ADD Z
460E 0102	STO X

Notice: (a) how much simpler it is to program in a high-level language

and (b) how much detail must be considered when programming in machine code, e.g. the actual memory addresses 0100, 0101 and 0102 for Y, Z and X must be noted, and the exact bit combination in hexadecimal form must be recorded for the operator part of each instruction.

The method of program entry is variable. The easiest technique is to use a keyboard for entry for whatever programming level is being applied. The compiler, assembler or loader program which already resides in memory will then respond to a numerical display or VDU with the entered characters.

An alternative technique is to compile, assemble or load the program on to a floppy disc, paper tape, or other storage medium, and finally load the program in machine-code form into memory for program running as a separate process.

If the program is to be loaded into ROM rather than RAM then this must be performed offline using some sort of development or production facility.

It is worth while emphasising that microcomputer software has not advanced at anything like the rate of microcomputer hardware technology. Software facilities for microcomputers lag far behind those for minicomputers in terms of compilers and assemblers, operating systems (i.e. system organiser programs) and utility programs which make the job of the programmer easier. For example, many microcomputer assemblers assemble entered instructions one at a time. This is not as convenient as assembling when the entire program is entered after an editing process on the source program has been carried out. Also most microcomputer compilers compile the program at run time and are called "interpreters". This is not as convenient as compiling the program after it is entered and storing the machine-code version. When the machine-code program is subsequently run it will run faster without the necessity for an additional compile process before each run.

An assembler which assembles each line as it is entered is often called an "interpreter".

Finally it is worth while mentioning some of the most popular high-level languages which are used for microcomputers. BASIC, FORTRAN, PASCAL and others are applied, although BASIC is the most commonly used. Other languages which are applied more in minicomputers and mainframes are ALGOL, COBOL, CORAL, etc.

7.3 DEVELOPMENT FACILITIES

The implementation of a process monitoring and control system requires the process of program testing and finally the implementation of the program onto PROM or EPROM. The value of using EPROM is that program modifications can be easily implemented without the necessity to discard updated PROMs. EPROMs are re-usable. Note that in a large floppy or hard disc system it is possible to store the system program on backing store. The program is then loaded into RAM for system run.

A development facility is required for the testing of programs and the final PROM "blowing" operation. Such a system is shown in Figure 7.1. The CPU and memory normally represent the most

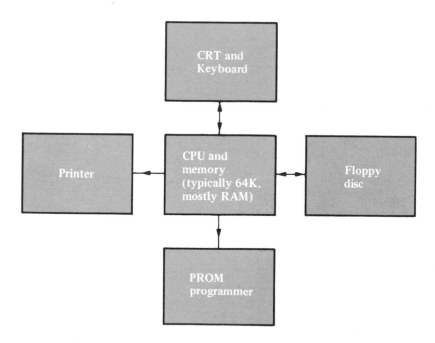

Figure 7.1 Microprocessor Development System

powerful configuration which is possible, i.e. maximum memory is utilised with most of memory being held in RAM to enable program compilation or assembly and testing. The programmer enters his program via the keyboard and CRT. The program can be at any language level—high level, assembler or even machine code. However, he would be unlikely to deviate from the use of a high-level language unless fast scanning routines or complex bit-handling routines are required.

The floppy disc stores his entered program, probably in both source and object code. The compiler programs and other utilities are also stored on floppy.

The printer is used primarily to produce a hard copy of entered programs.

When the testing procedure is complete the programmer will demand that his program in machine code shall be written into PROM or EPROM using the PROM Programmer. An offline device—a U.V. Eraser—is necessary if old EPROMs are to be re-utilised.

There are two program development facilities which greatly ease the programmer's job:

(a) TEXT EDITOR. This is used for both high-level language and assembler programs. It enables the programmer to enter his program then modify, insert and delete program lines as required. This avoids the necessity for complete program re-entry if a correction has to be made.

(b) IN-CIRCUIT EMULATION. This is not an easy facility to use but it is the most sophisticated design and debugging tool which is available. It is a combined hardware–software facility in which the microprocessor chip is removed from the prototype system under test. A cable from the development system is plugged in its place, and the development system can then completely control and monitor the system (memory, input/output, but excluding removed CPU) under test.

The name of the program which services the operator's keyboard and calls any compiler, interpreter, or assembler programs in development systems or training systems is the MONITOR. The monitor is normally ROM-based. Some development systems include a cross-assembler. This enables a program for a different microprocessor to be entered and assembled into machine code for the different machine type.

7.4 EXECUTIVE ROUTINES

Most single function microcomputer applications employ a single simple program. This may be complicated slightly if an interrupt facility is required.

A multi-programming application requires some sort of master organiser program which controls all of the others. In a large minicomputer application such a program tends to be called an "Operating System" or the "Executive". Essentially it is not really a single program but it consists of a series of small programs or routines which handle specific functions.

In a microcomputer system which has several peripherals and a plant interface, an operating system will have to handle the following functions:

(a) *Program scheduling,* i.e. it must be able to handle the calling of a program either from another program or on a timed basis. For example, a program which is scanning the plant interface may wish to call a printer program only if a plant measurement is in alarm. Timed calls for programs can be on a regular timed basis, e.g. every second call the plant interface scan program, every minute send data to a remote computer, or on a delayed timed basis, e.g. wait 100 msec for multiplexing relays to settle then call the program to read digital inputs. Programs can be called in this manner by number or by specifying the actual memory (or backing store) address at which the program resides. If called by number or even name, the program scheduler has to look-up the program address before calling it.

(b) *Backing store control,* i.e. read and write operations to floppy or hard disc. In this case the system program which requires a disc transfer presents the specification of the transfer to the disc-control routine. It normally does this by placing disc address and read/write marker in a buffer area in memory (RAM). The executive routine then handles the transfer and returns control to the calling program when complete. In this way a block of data which is held on disc can be read or written to by the system program, e.g. for storing historical plant data, or accessing printer messages.

(c) *Keyboard servicing and CRT driving.* Keyboard scanning is a frequently run routine, e.g. every 10 msec, so that the operation of a key is not missed. Alternatively the operation of a serial drive keyboard could be on interrupt. The driving of a CRT which can be in the form of a direct video drive to a TV monitor or a serial drive to a VDU is of two types. The video drive requires only the correct setting of the memory mapped video in RAM, but the VDU drive requires the sequential transmission of ASCII characters. In this latter case the system program will place the ASCII data in a memory buffer area and call the serial drive routine to handle the timing of the transmission process.

(d) *Other serial link drives,* i.e. printer and data link (to other computers) drives. These will normally be handled in the same way as the VDU drive.

(e) *Plant interface scanning,* i.e. analogue and digital input scanning and analogue and digital output setting. This function is often considered as one of the system programs and as such would be called on a timed basis. Alternatively if a fairly standard input/output configuration is applied, it is more realistic to view the plant interface program as an executive routine which places scanned inputs into a buffer area of memory and samples and sends from a different memory area for outputs. Thus system programs such as display programs and control programs use these buffer areas and trust the executive routine to continually place the latest input readings there and to immediately update output signals to plant from the corresponding output area.

(f) *Timing control* for all of these functions. For a powerful programming system of this type it is necessary to "clock" the operating system with real time kicks. This is to enable the regular time call functions and to maintain a time-of-day clock. This is normally performed by using an interrupt line as a timer, with an accurate external timing circuit generating an interrupt perhaps every 10 msec. The executive routine which is called to service these interrupts then updates the system time in memory and checks to see if any time or delay call is now required.

7.5 UTILITY MODULES

The following small utility programs are useful for both development situations and for operational systems:

(a) *Memory access.* The simplest monitor program and the most powerful operating system will possess the facility of indicating to the operator the contents of memory locations. This could be on a CRT or on a decimal LED display. This is particularly useful when fault finding at the development or operational stage and enables data and program instructions to be examined. It is helpful to have the facility to alter memory contents (RAM only, of course). Similarly it is useful to be able to display and alter files on floppy or hard disc; the display of a complete block of data is particularly helpful.

(b) *Dump*. A utility program which dumps a program or data file in ROM, RAM or backing store to paper tape, printer, magnetic tape cassette or floppy disc enables a secure copy to be filed for security purposes. This is useful for programs, message text files, CRT screen formats, historical plant data files, etc.

(c) *Reload*. A corresponding loader program which handles the re-load of such files to RAM or floppy/hard disc provides the facility of re-establishing programs or data files which may become corrupted or outdated.

(d) *Backing store mapping*. This utility would only be required if a large number of programs and data files are held on backing store. It would provide typically a display or printout of the layout and sizes of programs and data files (probably indicated by name or number) on backing store.

7.6 SCANNING ROUTINES

The plant interface scanning routines may be considered as part of the executive routines or as separate system programs. In any case it is worth while emphasising their main features here.

7.6.1 Analogue input scanning

Unless analogue input signals have to be scanned very rapidly for control purposes it is not worth while scanning for process logging and display more than once every few seconds. Normally the entire list, from a handful to several hundred, will be scanned one after the other. A small settling time is necessary between each channel scan in a multiplexed system. The processing stages which are necessary in handling the A/D counts are:

(a) *Scaling*—to produce engineering units (e.g. temperature in degrees C from a count reading). Note that it is often useful to store the raw count in memory and allow any user programs (display, control, logging, data link) to convert to engineering units.

$$\text{Engineering units} = \frac{\text{Count}}{\text{Max. count}} \times (\text{Scale max} - \text{Scale min}) + \text{Scale min}$$

(b) *Linearising*—a linearising routine may be necessary to correct for a non-linear thermocouple reading or to handle a square-root relationship to convert DP (differential pressure) to flow.

(c) *Offset correction*—a 0–10-V signal does not require offset correction, but a 4–20-mA signal which is converted to 2–10 V by applying a 500-Ω terminating resistor does require offset correction.

(d) *Alarm checking*—the A/D count, or the value expressed in engineering units, can be compared against stored limits and a marker set. This marker can cause an alarm routine to produce a printer message, sound an audible alarm or flash a message on a CRT.

7.6.2 Digital input scanning

The only rule about scanning digital input signals is that scanning must be fast enough to prevent any signal change going undetected. This may require scanning the range of digital inputs every 100 or every 10 msec. It is common to scan all digital inputs and update a reserved area of memory with the state of the signals so that system programs can easily observe the latest readings. Also it is customary in the scanning process to call a system program immediately when an important bit corresponding to a particular plant signal changes, e.g. pulsed inputs which have to be counted, emergency stop pushbutton, valve operation, controller mode change, etc.

7.6.3 Analogue and digital output setting

A convenient method of making analogue and digital output changes is for system programs to set the required settings into a memory buffer area. The output routines then examine this area, compare with a mirror area which indicated the previous output states and implements changes as necessary.

7.7 CALCULATION ROUTINES

Apart from the more obvious calculation routines, e.g. summing two instrument readings, totalising flows or weights, etc., other more specialised calculations sometimes have to be performed. This can be done by setting a calculation marker and calculation number in the specification data for analogue inputs, such that the required calculation routine is called after that value is scanned. Examples are:

7.7.1 Flow calculation

$$\text{Flow} = \sqrt[K]{\frac{DP}{P \times T}}$$

where DP = differential pressure,
$\quad$ *P* = pressure,
$\quad$ *T* = temperature,
$\quad$ *K* = constant.

7.7.2 Hot-dip thermocouple plateau detection

The signal from a thermocouple which is used for measuring very high temperatures, e.g. 1000 to 1800°C for molten metal, will rise to the appropriate level, settle for a few seconds and then either collapse to zero, when the thermocouple or connecting cable burns out, or reduce as the thermocouple is withdrawn. In this latter process the thermocouple reading may well increase to a sharp peak if the device is withdrawn through higher temperature slag which floats on the metal surface.

A simple routine must scan this reading on a regular basis once the reading starts to rise; this is normally triggered by a digital input from the thermocouple amplifier/recorder system which represents "temperature rising". The scanning speed for that particular channel may well have to be increased (say once per second) during this period. The program must detect the "plateau", i.e. the largest flat part of the characteristic in order to read the temperature accurately.

7.7.3 Averaging several readings

A simpler type of calculation routine may be required to sum and then average several readings which are of a similar type. For example, the average of several pressures in a service-supply system may be required, or more commonly several thermocouples may be used in a particularly harsh environment such that measurement can be maintained in the event of the failure of one or two thermocouples. In this latter case readings which represent failed transducers must be excluded from the calculation.

This last point raises the issue of instrument availability. What should the scanning routine and system programs do if an instrument fails? The scanning routine may be able to detect failure on its own, e.g. reading is zero on a 4–20-mA range, or the operator may make a keyboard or switch entry to indicate the unavailability of the instrument. It may be sensible for the scanning routine to exclude that instrument from its scanning list. What is more important, however, is what the display, logging and control programs should do with the faulty reading.

The options are:

(a) Keep scanning and use the faulty reading, which is probably zero.

(b) Stop scanning but use the last scanned value, which could be sensible if the scanning routine was triggered by manual entry to stop scanning before the reading failed, e.g. instrument switched off or removed for servicing.

(c) Use a standby "guesstimate" value.

(d) use a manually entered reading, which should be updated regularly by the operator.

The last option is best.

7.8 DISPLAY PROGRAMMING

7.8.1 Direct video

The specification of the graphical or textual format of the screen is made using high level language statements, e.g.

PLOT 0,3 TO 20,3

which causes a line to be drawn on row 3 of the screen from column 0 to 20, or

PRINT "ALARM READINGS"

which cause the text "ALARM READINGS" to be displayed.

The mechanism by which these statements are converted into bits which are set into the memory-mapped area for direct video drive is that the interpreter or compiler uses calls on subroutines which perform this conversion process.

Thus a few high-level language statements can cause a detailed drawing (plant mimic, text display) to be formatted into the memory area which holds the video bit pattern.

The addition of alphanumeric (letters and numbers) information to a full graphics display is often required, e.g. to add numerical instrumentation data to a plant mimic. The method of performing this is again to use a special subroutine which is called by the interpreter or compiler. This subroutine is given a "shape table" to insert the appropriate bits into the memory-mapped area in order to display the required character.

7.8.2 VDU display

Section 7.4 (c) described how an executive routine picks up the ASCII characters from a memory buffer and transmits them serially. The system program which generates the screen format places the ASCII characters in this buffer by using subroutines. For example, the high-level statement

SOP (2,0 "INSTRUMENT DATA")

says output the text string "INSTRUMENT DATA" to be displayed on line 2, starting at column 0. The SOP command causes a sub-routine to place these text characters into the buffer area at a position which corresponds to the screen position. For example, if the screen is 64 characters wide by 20 rows, then 64 characters will be required for each of 20 rows giving a total number of characters of $64 \times 20 = 1280$. This complete list of 1280 characters must be serially transmitted each time the screen is updated. Note that at a slow baud rate of 1200, a screen update will take approximately 10 seconds. This is the main reason for maximising baud rates. Even more characters must be transmitted if a colour VDU is used in order to specify colour changes.

Several VDUs possess a "semi-graphics" facility, i.e. graphical shapes can be approximated using non-alphanumeric characters. The characters are chosen so that straight lines, curves and process shapes (e.g. valves, arrows, pipe angles) can be created. These characters are handled by the system display program and the executive driver program in the same way as the normal alphanumeric characters. The method of adding dynamic plant data readings numerically to a semigraphics plant mimic display is relatively simple. The ASCII characters for the decimal numbers are inserted into the appropriate places in the line-column matrix of characters which is held in memory. The remote VDU converts the serially received screen characters into the video drive signal of course.

7.9 DATA STORAGE

An 8-bit microprocessor handles "number crunching", i.e. extensive arithmetic operations, very slowly. If only 8 bits are used to represent numbers and the most significant bit represents the sign of the number then clearly very little accuracy and number range are possible, viz. from −128 to +128.

The use of 16 bit numbers extends the range to −32,768 to +32,768. This is simply achieved when using 16-bit microprocessors, but involves considerable processing when performed by software in an 8-bit microprocessor.

Sometimes it is required to represent numbers beyond this range. The method of achieving this is to use FLOATING POINT NUMBERS. A 16-bit floating point number (625,000) looks like:

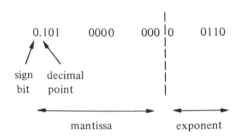

The mantissa is $0.5 + 0.125 = 0.625$. The exponent is 6 and tells us how many places the decimal point of the mantissa must be shifted, i.e. 0.625 shifted right 6 places $= 625,000$

If the exponent was negative the shifting would be in the opposite direction. 32-bit operation produces greater accuracy and is more common.

Software routines are required to perform arithmetic using these numbers, and this produces very slow but accurate number manipulation.

When a backing store is used in a system it is often difficult to decide where data (in integer, i.e. normal, form or floating point form) should be stored. A sensible choice is normally that regularly used data, e.g. constants, scaling factors, alarm limits, etc., should be stored in RAM, but historical data, which is used for trend display or summarising logs, should be stored on backing store. A list of current readings of plant instruments, controllers, digital input states, etc., must also be held in RAM for fast access.

Non-numerical data, e.g. text for logs and display formats, should also be held on backing store.

7.10 SYSTEM LOADING

In a small ROM-based application, the system program will re-start conveniently on its own when the machine is switched on. This is achieved using a "Power-up" interrupt which causes a re-start routine in ROM to run and set up whatever data is required in RAM. This routine then transfers control into the main system program.

If a large area of RAM has to be filled with program and data, then a load facility off floppy disc, hard disc or even magnetic-tape cassette may be used. This is particularly relevant in the case of a system which possesses several programs which are stored on backing store. The short program which is called by the power-up interrupt to perform this system set-up is often called a BOOTSTRAP LOADER. The bootstrap loader could be:

(a) ROM-based, i.e. the power-up interrupt enters this routine directly.

(b) Backing store based, i.e. the power-up interrupt enters a small loader routine which performs a backing store transfer to read down the loader program; this program performs system set-up and then transfers control to the main system program (the operating system).

7.11 HARDWARE DIAGNOSTIC ROUTINES

The components in a microcomputer system beyond the CPU and memory tend to introduce most of the overall unreliability. Electro-mechanical peripherals and the plant interface yield most faults and it is useful to have some means of testing these devices.

Some peripherals often have their own self-test facilities which are activated on switch-on and exercise most of the internal equipment. Such devices are printers and plotters. It is useful to have a means of testing these devices also from the computer so that the data link is also tested. A standard alphanumeric printout in the case of a printer and a text and shape plot routine for the plotter are satisfactory diagnostic facilities.

It is convenient to call these facilities from a keyboard. A VDU test display is also a useful test feature.

A facility to test the backing store is less frequently applied. A rigorous test would be to write bit patterns over all tracks of the device and read back and check these patterns. Naturally this test must not be performed if the backing store information must be preserved. Notice that many backing store devices include some form of error detection in their hardware, e.g. the self-address of a track record is stored together with the data, and this self-address is checked on read operations.

A test panel or keyboard and display facility can be supplied to monitor plant interface signals individually. Thus the readings of analogue and digital inputs can be checked. Care must be taken if output signals are tested online in order to avoid inadvertently switching on or off a remote piece of equipment.

FURTHER READING

1. Hartley, M.G., and Healey, M., *A First Course in Computer Technology*, McGraw-Hill, New York and London, 1978.
2. Higman, B., *A Comparative Study of Programming Languages*, Macdonald, London, 1970.
3. Palmer, D.C. and Morris, B.D., *Computing Science*, Edward Arnold, London, 1980.
4. Agdin, C.A., *Software Design for Microcomputers*, Prentice-Hall, London, 1978.
5. Streitmatter, G.A., *Microprocessor Software*, Prentice-Hall, London, 1981.

Chapter 8

Applications

8.1 DISTRIBUTED PROCESSING SYSTEM

A large process monitoring and control system which uses minicomputers and microcomputers at the British Steel Corporation Works at Port Talbot is shown in Figure 8.1.

This system has been completely engineered and programmed by B.S.C. development staff. It consists of nine minicomputers and thirteen microcomputers and performs a comprehensive range of plant monitoring and control functions. In addition production, technical and stock-control logging functions are performed. It should be emphasised that the size of this system is atypical, but it is an indication of how diverse and extensive distributed processing systems can become.

The blocks above the dotted line in the diagram are all Ferranti Argus 700 minicomputers; several models within this range are represented. The blocks below the dotted line are all microcomputers which interface directly to plant. Indeed this division indicates the philosophy behind the design of the system. In general, microcomputers handle data collection from plant and some output-control functions, whilst minicomputers handle the more onerous functions of plant data filing, operator VDU driving and data-link driving to the main Area Minicomputer. The Area Computer is the largest in the system and uses a 10-megabyte removable cartridge disc for data filing. It is backed-up with a standby computer which also possesses a disc. A shared third disc provides additional security and enables data files and new programs to be passed between computers. Apart from producing production logs on a daily and longer term basis and technical logs, etc., the Area Computer routes all data flow around the network.

An example of this data transmission feature is the link to the British Rail TOPS freight computer which transmits advisings of coal deliveries to the Area Computer. Individual weights of coal wagons

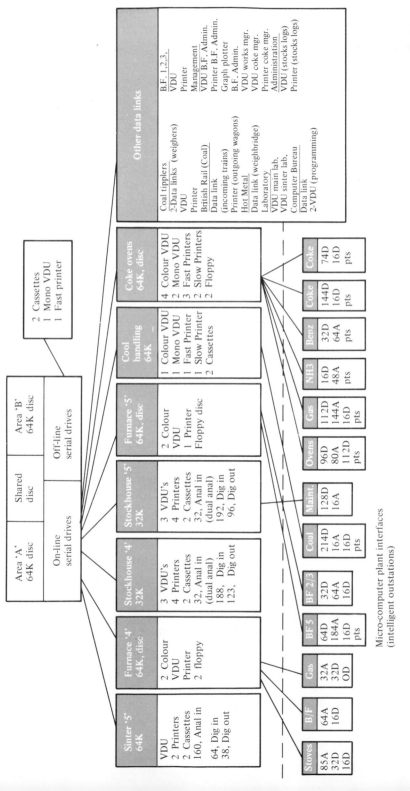

FIGURE 8.1 DISTRIBUTED PROCESSING SYSTEM FOR AN IRONWORKS

are transmitted from a weighbridge at the works discharge point so that the Area Computer can check deliveries against advisings. A printer link back to British Rail indicates the release of wagons.

The central works analysing laboratory analyses all raw materials and products of the various ironmaking processes. In fact individual analyser microcomputers assist this process, although this system is not shown on the diagram. Analyses are then entered by VDU to the Area Computer for filing and logging purposes and retransmission to the individual process Logger Computers.

The main level of minicomputers consists of units which perform plant monitoring mainly with the use of colour VDUs. Some remote switching-control facilities are also included. The VDU displays give operators centralised monitoring and control of their particular plant with the use of plant mimic, trend, instrument data and alarm displays (examples were given in Chapter 5). Instrument specifications, new mimics and log format changes can all be implemented online.

Within this group of minicomputers are two machines which perform direct sequence and charging control functions; these are blast furnace 4 and 5 stockhouse computers.

One of these is backed-up with a microcomputer PLC (programmable logic controller). These minicomputers are monochrome VDU machines.

Apart from the sinter plant Logger Computer, which is an early machine and possesses its own plant interface, the other logger minicomputers obtain their plant interface via serial links to outstation microcomputers. These microcomputers carry analogue and digital input/output equipment to monitor plant operation (via instruments and contact closure signals).

In the following sections 8.2, 8.3 and 8.4 we will examine the operation of some of these microcomputer systems in more detail.

8.2 OUTSTATIONS

Several manufacturers produce microprocessor-based systems for data collection from plant and serial drive capability to remote computers. Control facilities could also be programmed into these machines.

Prices are not low, typically £10,000 to £25,000, but large numbers of signals can be handled. A large configuration may offer a system with a capacity of 512 analogue and/or digital signals.

A philosophy of equipment configuration is based on the use of "micro-modules". These are simply small PCBs (printed circuit boards) which perform specific functions. They are slotted into box positions in a particular combination to produce the required configuration of analogue and digital inputs and outputs.

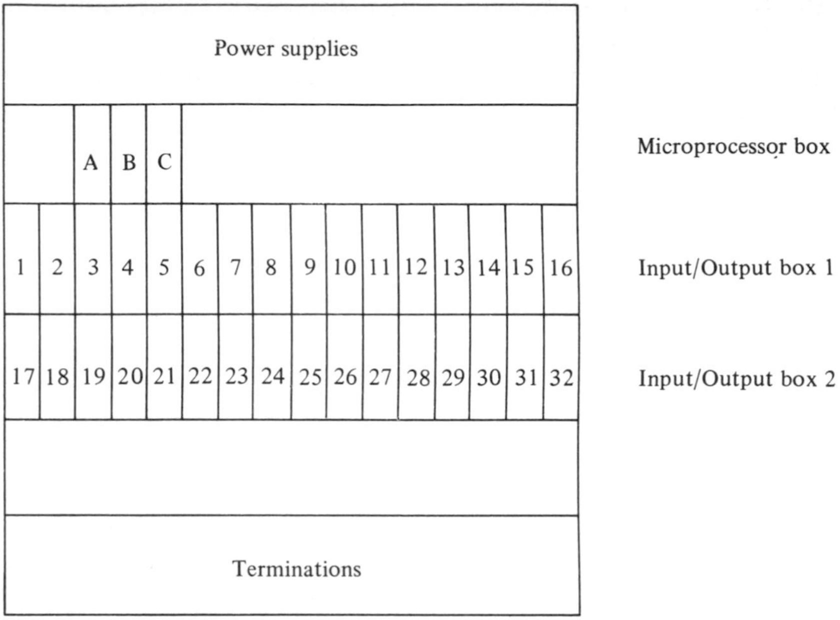

FIGURE 8.2 TYPICAL MICRO-MEDIA CUBICLE

Figure 8.2 shows a typical outstation. The individual boards fall into the following categories:

(a) A 3-board combination A, B and C provide the microprocessor and memory board, a serial link-drive board (to a remote minicomputer) and a control board for communication to the input/output boxes below.

(b) A 16-channel analogue input multiplexor board plus an A/D board in a 2-board combination can form any adjacent board pair in slots 1 to 32.

(c) A 16-digital inputs board. Integrated circuit opto-isolators are used and multiplexing is not applied.

(d) A 16-digital outputs board, again using opto-isolators.

(e) Analogue output boards are also available.

Additional signals and boards to handle them can be added by wiring to vacant slot positions in the input/output boxes. In this case the PROM program which holds a "map" of the particular board configuration for that outstation will then have to be reprogrammed. This system program has two primary functions:

(i) to scan the input boards and update the output board via a RAM data list;

(ii) to communicate input and output signals to a remote computer by serial link.

The connection between the microprocessor box and the input/output boxes is via a bus system of data lines, address lines and control signals. Not shown in Figure 8.2 are the driver boards within each box to handle this bus connection.

8.3 SEQUENCE CONTROL

Two of the sequence and switching control machines in the large configuration of Figure 8.1 are minicomputers, but a microcomputer system provides a back-up facility for one of them. In any case the description which follows is a general summary of the facilities which are available on the new ranges of microcomputer PLCs.

The equipment configuration is not dissimilar to that of the outstation which was just described. The plant interface is predominantly if not totally digital. A small CRT is available to display the electrical circuit analogy of the sequence which the microprocessor performs and to enable modified and new sequence to be entered.

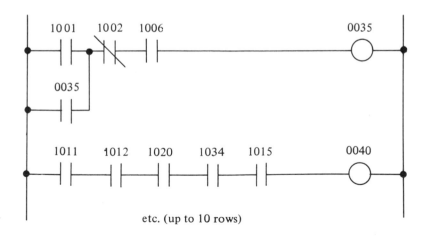

etc. (up to 10 rows)

FIGURE 8.3 LADDER NETWORK DISPLAY FOR MICROCOMPUTER PLC

Figure 8.3 shows a typical CRT display of a simple logic system or sequence control system. The analagous components in an electrical equivalent circuit are as follows (electrical engineers should be well acquainted with these concepts):

   (a) The circle on the right of each row represents a relay or contactor coil which it is required to energise as a result of a series of contact closures.

   (b) The contact closures are shown with the capacitor symbol. A diagonal line across this symbol indicates that it is normally closed.

Digital inputs are referenced with a 4-digit number, with the first digit set to 1. Digital outputs, which are set only when the equivalent series electrical circuit is made, are referenced with the first digit set to 0.

Notice that a digital output signal can also cause a dummy digital input signal to be set, e.g. output 0035 has an associated dummy input 0035. This is analagous to the common start/stop latch circuit which was described in section 3.12.

As each simulated contact closure signal is set from left to right across each horizontal series circuit, the circuit up to that point is illuminated on the screen with an increased intensity.

The CRT is therefore used to indicate the operation of each logic circuit and enables the sequence to be monitored. Additionally the CRT and keyboard are used to specify a logic sequence, i.e. the system can be designed using a standard program package and no special programming is necessary.

The format of the display is called a "ladder network" and typically ten rows of ten series contacts are available.

8.4 PUSHING-CAR POSITION LOGGING

A highly tailored and novel application which is under current development is the system which provides information to one of the logging computers in Figure 8.1.

A pushing car travels along a track in front of a battery of coke ovens, and every 10 minutes or so pushes the charge out of the specified oven. The microcomputer system, which is mounted on the car, provides a ground station with information concerning the position of the car and other data. This information is then transmitted serially to the logging minicomputer.

Figure 8.4 shows how the pushing car moves along its track in front of the oven wall. The aerial on the car is continuously transmitting a fixed frequency signal. This is detected and amplified by only one of the transponders which are mounted on the oven wall. Thus as the car

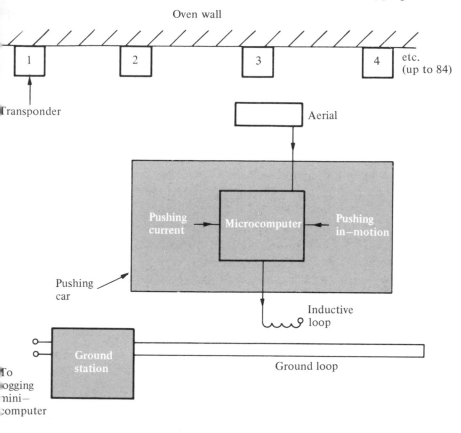

FIGURE 8.4 PUSHING CAR POSITION LOGGING SYSTEM

is positioned in front of just one oven, the transponder for only that oven can rectify the transmitted signal and use that d.c. power to energise a circuit which re-transmits an identity number. This transponder technique of providing power and then receiving a "badge number" is the identical system which is used for tracking the locations of buses and the new high-speed trains (the transponders are mounted on the moving vehicles).

The microcomputer, which is Z80 based, reads this oven number via a digital input interface from the aerial circuit. Further inputs scan the pushing current (analogue) and pushing-in-motion (digital) signals. A composite message is then prepared by the microcomputer program and used to modulate an a.c. carrier signal which passes through an inductive loop. The inductive loop and the receiver ground loop operate on the transformer principle. The ground station then re-transmits the serial message in RS232C form to the minicomputer.

When the pushing car therefore is driven to a position in front of one of the eighty-four ovens, and pushes that oven, a message is assembled and sent to the logger computer. This computer can use this information for oven sequence control and general production data logging.

8.5 WATER-TURBINE GOVERNOR

The North of Scotland Hydro Electric Board and Glasgow University have developed a microprocessor-based speed controller (governor) of a hydroturbine which supplies electrical power to the National Grid. Conventional electronics systems aim to make the governor more responsive to the demands of the grid, but the microprocessor solution offers more flexibility and permits the implementation of complex control strategies.

The microcomputer governor adjusts the position of the water-control valve in response to changes in turbine speed. Additional control actions are implemented to limit the load to prevent over-acceleration and to provide a basic valve servo position setpoint.

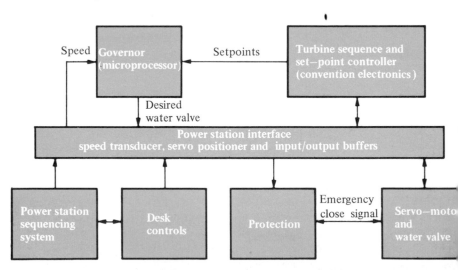

FIGURE 8.5 MICROCOMPUTER WATER TURBINE GOVERNOR

The general equipment configuration is shown in Figure 8.5. The microcomputer governor scans three setpoints (speed, servo position and load limit) and one speed reading. An analogue output signal drives the water valve. The conventional turbine sequence and power station sequencing and protection equipment handle the traditional control systems. This equipment uses signal conditioning circuitry before connection to the microcomputer.

The governor microcomputer comprises:

(a) An Intel SBC (single-board computer) 80/10 processor board—this is 8080 based and includes 4 K EPROM and 1 K RAM.

(b) Analog devices RTI 1200 analogue input/output board.

(c) National semiconductors BLC 84/32, 16 K EPROM board.

The system program was developed in FORTRAN on an Intel 230 MDS (microprocessor development system). Extensive use of an in-circuit emulator was applied when testing the developed program in the prototype SBC 80/10 board.

This application demonstrates a small plant interface but a well-researched and complex control program.

8.6 PERSONAL COMPUTER FOR PROCESS CONTROL

The normal microcomputer system for a process monitoring or control application consists of the following typical "micro-modules" (individual boards):

(a) A microprocessor, ROM and RAM board.

(b) Extension ROM and RAM board.

(c) RS232C serial drive board.

(d) Floppy-disc drive board.

(e) Display drive board.

(f) Digital input card (perhaps 32 isolated inputs).

(g) Analogue input card (perhaps 16 inputs).

(h) Digital output card (perhaps 32 isolated outputs).

(i) Analogue output card (perhaps 16 outputs).

Each board may cost from £100 to £500 and the housing box/cubicle with power supplies may cost £1000. Thus even a small system could cost several thousand pounds. Additionally a development system is necessary for program development, e.g. edit, assemble, compile, file handling, PROM blowing, etc. This can cost from £3000 to £10,000.

A personal computer is not designed as a process control machine. However, it is cheap, possesses convenient program-testing facilities and has good display features. Its high-level language programs (normally BASIC) run in an interpretive mode and are consequently slow in operation. However, if speed is not a system requirement and a

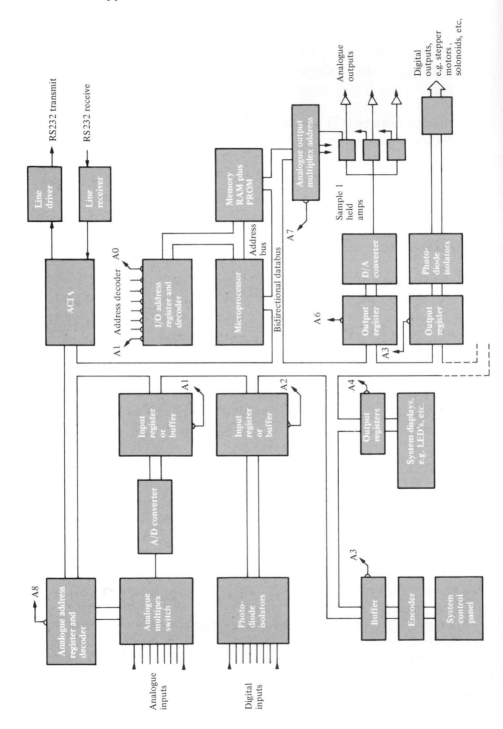

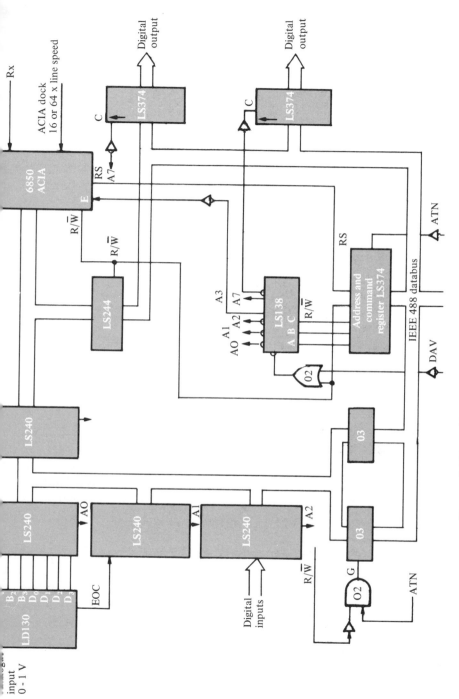

FIGURE 8.7 INPUT/OUTPUT BOARD WITH IEEE 488 INTERFACE

small plant interface can be built into the machine, it is possible to use a personal computer for a process-control application. If a time-critical function is required, this can be programmed in assembly code, and linked with a slow but powerful display program. The general requirement is for a system as shown in Figure 8.6.

The Commodore PET just leads the Apple II as the most popular personal computer. It is based on the 6502 microprocessor and has up to 32 K RAM, a VDU and keyboard and a floppy-disc drive. It possesses a BASIC interpreter. It generates an IEEE 488 interface for connecting additional boards to the system. One such board which possesses analogue and digital input/output circuitry is shown in Figure 8.7.

The IEEE 488 data bus from the PET enters the board at the bottom of the circuit schematic. This open collector bus represents both data and input/output addresses. The setting of the ATN line identifies information on the bus as data or address. DAV is a timing control signal.

The 74LS138 is the address decode chip (see section 2.10.1 for a description of the principle of operation). One of A0 to A7 is set to provide the CHIP SELECT signal to one of the input/output chips. The 74LS374 chips are 8-bit registers which staticise data, e.g. for the digital outputs. The 74LS240 chips are simply 8-bit tristate buffer packages and are used for digital inputs and analogue inputs (following A/D conversion in the LD130). Analogue outputs are not shown but could be added simply with the use of D/A chips. The 6850 is a UART for serial communication to an external device.

Input/output is memory mapped and so programming is straightforward using BASIC PEEK (input) and POKE (output) instructions. Machine code routines and BASIC display programs can be readily implemented to perform a simple process monitoring or control function.

Such a system has been applied in a small process-control application. The major disadvantages are the need to input commands to load and run the control program when the machine is switched on, the slow run speed of a program under the BASIC interpreter and the need to maintain a clean and electrically noise-free environment. The advantages are cost (especially for a single system) and the simplicity of screen formatting and program entry.

FURTHER READING

1. Grant, N.F., Aitken, K.H., Winning, D.J. and Davie, H., Development of an operational hydroturbine governor, *Microprocessors and Microsystems,* Vol. 4, No. 9, Butterworth, Guildford, 1980.
2. Pritty, D. and Barrie, D., Personal computers in automation systems, *Microprocessors and Microsystems,* Vol. 5, No. 4, Butterworth, Guildford, 1981.
3. Weitzman, C., *Distributed Micro/Minicomputer Systems,* Prentice-Hall, London, 1980.

Chapter 9

Operating Details for Specific Microcomputers

9.1 THE APPLE II MICROCOMPUTER

9.1.1 Introduction

The Apple II is a mass-produced personal computer. It is well supported by a wide range of software packages for commercial and training application. Although it is designed only for an office environment, it could be used for small, low-power process-control applications.

Figure 9.1 shows the basic equipment configuration. The main Apple board supports an MOS Technology 6502 microprocessor, 14 K of ROM and 48 K of RAM. A second board handles the drive to the floppy-disc unit. A normal colour television receiver operates as the display device. Full graphics displays can be produced.

Programs can be entered via the keyboard in Basic or machine code. Program listings can be obtained on a serial drive printer.

Additional boards can be added to provide extra facilities, e.g. a small plant interface.

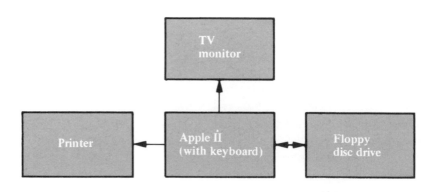

FIGURE 9.1 THE APPLE II MICROCOMPUTER

9.1.2 Memory map

Table 9.1 shows the layout of memory.

TABLE 9.1 APPLE II MEMORY MAP

Decimal	Hex		
0000 2047	0000 07FF	Reserved Data Area	(2 K)
2048 8191	0800 IFFF	BASIC Program	(6 K)
8192 16383	2000 3FFF	Page 1 — HGR (Picture Buffer)	(8 K)
16384 24575	4000 5FFF	Page 2 — HGR 2 (Picture Buffer)	(8 K)
24576 38015	6000 95FF	Spare	(13½ K)
38016 49151	9600 BFFF	DOS	(10½ K) RAM
49152 51199	C000 C7FF	Input/Output Addresses	(2 K)
51200 53247	C800 CFFF	Input/Output (ROM)	(2 K)
53248 65535	D000 FFFF	Monitor, BASIC Interpreter (ROM)	(12 K)

The first 2 K is reserved for the stack, interrupt vectors and data for text and low-resolution graphics displays.

A program which is entered in Basic is run in the next 6 K of memory.

The next two blocks of 8 K are used to hold the memory-mapped video data for the high-resolution graphics display feature. There are two pages of high-resolution displays. This provides a fast switching facility between displays.

13½ K of spare RAM memory follows. This can be used for data lists and machine code programs.

DOS, the Disc Operating System, uses the last 10½ K of RAM. This is the executive program which runs the Basic interpreter and the user's program and organises all floppy-disc transfers.

Following the 48 K of RAM addresses is 2 K of input/output addresses and 2 K of ROM which is used input/output transfers.

Finally 12 K of ROM holds the Monitor program and Basic interpreter. The type of Basic language which is used is called Applesoft Basic.

9.1.3 Text display

Consider a simple display of text plus some numerical data, e.g. a display of instruments in alarm, or a display of average readings for the last hour.

Figure 9.2 shows a typical text display and Table 9.2 lists the program which has to be entered in Basic to achieve this format. Notice that each program line is labelled numerically. Lines are numbered as multiples of 10 in order to leave space in case additional lines are inserted at a later time.

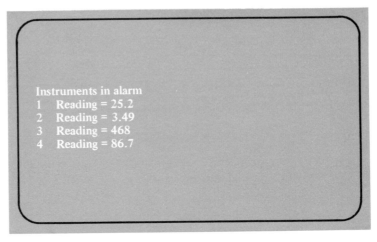

FIGURE 9.2 APPLE TEXT DISPLAY

The particular features of these Applesoft Basic lines are:

LINE 10 —REM refers to "remark" and the text which follows is for information only—it is not compiled.

LINE 30 —This sets a variable name R1 to 25.2.

LINE 80 —The HOME command clears the screen.

LINE 90 —TEXT is a special command which tells the Basic Interpreter that the following display commands are for text display (cf. HGR for high-resolution graphics display—described later).

LINE 100 —The VTAB command causes the position of the next line which is to be displayed on the screen to tab (shift) 10 lines downwards.

LINE 110 —The PRINT command causes the text which follows to be displayed.

LINE 130 —On this line there are two display (PRINT) commands. The semicolon separates them and the second PRINT is not required.

LINE 170 —The END command terminates the program.

TABLE 9.2 BASIC PROGRAM TO DISPLAY TEXT

```
 10  REM PROGRAM TO DISPLAY INSTRUMENTS IN ALARM
 20  REM SET UP ALARM READINGS
 30  R1 = 25.2
 40  R2 = 3.49
 50  R3 = 468
 60  R4 = 86.7
 70  REM DISPLAY HEADING
 80  HOME
 90  TEXT
100  VTAB 10
110  PRINT "INSTRUMENTS IN ALARM"
120  REM DISPLAY FOUR LINES OF ALARMS
130  PRINT "1    READING = ";R1
140  PRINT "2    READING = ";R2
150  PRINT "3    READING = ";R3
160  PRINT "4    READING = ";R4
170  END
```

The program is repeated in Table 9.3 with a program loop replacing the four PRINT lines. This is accomplished using the Basic commands FOR and NEXT (lines 130 and 150).

TABLE 9.3 BASIC PROGRAM TO DISPLAY TEXT (USING LOOP)

```
 10  REM PROGRAM TO DISPLAY INSTRUMENTS IN ALARM
 20  REM SET UP ALARM READINGS
 30  R(0) = 25.2
 40  R(1) = 3.49
 50  R(2) = 468
 60  R(3) = 86.7
 70  REM DISPLAY HEADING
 80  HOME
 90  TEXT
100  VTAB 10
110  PRINT "INSTRUMENTS IN ALARM"
120  REM DISPLAY FOUR LINES OF ALARMS
130  FOR I = 0 TO 3
140  PRINT I+1;"   READING = ";R(I)
150  NEXT
160  END
```

9.1.4 High-resolution graphics display

Low-resolution graphics displays can be created, but they are not as useful for displaying detailed plant mimics, etc., as are high-resolution graphics displays and consequently they will not be described here.

When displaying text the screen is divided into 40 columns by 24 rows. In high resolution graphics mode the screen has 280 by 160 plotting points. Additionally 4 rows at the bottom of the screen are available for text. Lines can be drawn between any two points on this matrix in any one of eight colours, as follows:

0 = black 1	4 = black 2
1 = green	5 = orange
2 = violet	6 = blue
3 = white 1	7 = white 2

A program which draws a simple plant mimic is shown in Table 9.4.

TABLE 9.4 BASIC PROGRAM TO DISPLAY MIMIC (USING GRAPHICS)

```
10 REM PROGRAM TO DRAW PLANT MIMIC
20 HOME
30 HGR
40 REM DRAW PIPE IN ORANGE
50 HCOLOR = 5
60 HPLOT 0,140 TO 88,140
70 REM DRAW RECTANGULAR VESSEL IN BLUE
80 HCOLOR = 6
90 FOR I = 80 TO 150
100 HPLOT 90,I TO 115,I
110 NEXT
120 END
```

The mimic represents a horizontal pipe which connects to a rectangular-shaped vessel as shown in Figure 9.3. Notice:

LINE 30 —HGR selects high-resolution graphics mode (280 by 160) leaving 4 lines for text at the bottom. The screen is cleared to black, and page 1 of memory is displayed.
If HGR 2 is used the matrix is 280 by 192, no text space is reserved at the bottom, the screen is cleared and page 2 of memory is displayed.

LINE 50 —The choice of colour is made using the command HCOLOR.

LINE 60 —This HPLOT statement says: Plot from Column 0, Row 140 to Column 88, Row 140, i.e. a horizontal line.

LINES 90 to 110 — These lines plot a series of vertically adjoining horizontal lines of the same length in order to produce a rectangular block of colour (the plant vessel).

Large and detailed plant mimics, or any other type of graphical display, can be created in this way.

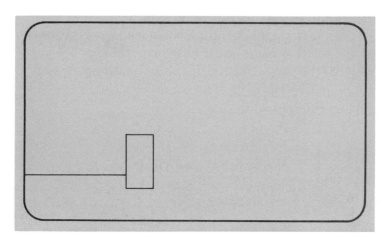

FIGURE 9.3 APPLE GRAPHICS DISPLAY

Alphanumeric text can be added in the bottom 4 lines of the screen. However, text cannot be inserted in the larger top part of the screen using the normal PRINT command. This can only be performed with the use of "shape tables". In this technique special software routines are called to implement Applesoft Basic commands. The actual shapes which are drawn are specified by the bit pattern which is held in a reserved data area in memory. For example, if the number 3 is to be drawn, and its specification is number 16 in the shape table,

DRAW 16 AT 100, 86

will cause the "3" shape to be drawn at column position 100 and row position 86. The routine which is called by DRAW transfers the definition of the shape to be transferred from the shape table to the memory mapped video area.

9.1.5 PEEK/POKE to memory and input/output

The PEEK and POKE commands in Basic enable data to be read from and written to memory and input/output.

For example:

VALUE = PEEK (24576) says place the contents of memory address 24576 in the variable VALUE.

Note: a variable name could be used in place of 24576.

NUMBER = PEEK (−16384) says place the contents of input/output address (65536–16384) in the variable NUMBER.

The minus sign differentiates between memory and input/output. Notice that −16384 is the first input/output address, and in fact is the keyboard. 65536 is the top address of the 64 K address range.

POKE 24576,6 says place the number 6 in memory location 24576. A variable name could be used in place of 6.

POKE −15871,2 says send the number 2 to input/output address (65536 − 15871).

Useful input/output addresses are:

−16384 Keyboard
−16336 Loudspeaker
−15871 Analogue input multiplexed channel number
−15872 A/D count

A complete list is given in Table 9.5.

TABLE 9.5 COMPLETE LIST OF INPUT/OUTPUTS

Address	Description	
−16384	Keyboard	
−16336	Loudspeaker	
−16296	Bit 0 off	
−16295	Bit 0 on	
−16294	Bit 1 off	
−16293	Bit 1 on	Digital outputs (4 off)
−16292	Bit 2 off	
−16291	Bit 2 on	
−16290	Bit 3 off	
−16289	Bit 3 on	
−16287	Bit 0	
−16286	Bit 1	Digital inputs (3 off)
−16285	Bit 2	
−16284	Channel 0	
−16283	Channel 1	Analogue inputs (4 off)
−16282	Channel 2	(Pots and timing circuits)
−16281	Channel 3	
−16272	Rest Analogue Input Timers	
−15872	A/D Count	Analogue inputs (8 off)
−15871	Channel Number	(additional board)

9.1.6 Editor

After a program has been entered and perhaps also tested, alterations may be made as follows:

To display the program simply key in the command LIST and press RETURN.

To list a section of the program use:

LIST 10,50

which displays program lines 10 to 50.

To correct any line:

(a) Press ESC then either I(↑), J(←), K(→) and M(↓) to position cursor at *start* of line to be edited. Therefore normally press ESC and I, I . . . I,I,J to position correctly.

(b) Use → and REPT to position at required point in instruction. After entering corrections press REPT and → simultaneously until cursor passes last character in instruction (this may be on the next row of the display).

(c) Press RETURN.

9.1.7 Monitor

It is sometimes necessary to enter the Monitor if it is required to enter data into memory, e.g. a list of test data items, or a shape table.

The procedure is:

(a) CALL — 151   This calls the Monitor.

(b) A * prompt is displayed.

(c) Key in 9088 and press RETURN if 9088 is the address to be changed.

(d) The contents of 9088 are displayed by Monitor.

(e) Press RETURN to cause a block of 8 memory locations to be displayed.

(f) To enter data into 9088, key in *9088: 0A 00 16, etc., press RETURN and Hex 0A is stored in 9088, 00 in 9099, etc.

(g) When finished key in 0G and press RETURN to return to Organiser and Basic.

9.1.8 Summary of program loading and testing

The full procedure for loading, testing, running and storing a program is:

1. Computer switched off. Load discette, required surface and label upright, oval cutout towards rear of the disc drive. Close disc-drive door.

2. Switch on computer, and system boots and loads (put DOS into RAM).

3. Key in program, as described above.
4. Key in RUN and press RETURN to test.
5. Press RESET to return to Organiser and Applesoft BASIC.
6. If program works correctly (unlikely!), give it a name (say HARRY) and save it on discette by keying SAVE HARRY and pressing RETURN.
7. Edit program, if necessary, as described above, re-test and save on discette when finished. A useful debugging tool which can be used after each run of the program is to key in ? TOM and press RETURN to examine the contents of the variable TOM.

The stored program can be subsequently run using RUN HARRY (and pressing RETURN), or it can be loaded from discette into RAM without being run (perhaps just for listing purposes) using LOAD HARRY (and pressing RETURN).

Notice that similar commands to SAVE and LOAD can be used with data files, which can be created using the Monitor (see section 9.1.7). For example, BSAVE SHAPE, A37000, L112
says save the binary file called SHAPE on discette from memory address 37000 (decimal).
The length of the file is 112 (decimal).
BLOAD SHAPE causes DOS to reload the file into the specified memory location.

9.1.9 Additional BASIC features

The features of Basic which are described in this book are clearly only a sample of the full Basic language, and reference should be made to the Applesoft II Basic Manual for a more comprehensive summary. However, some of the most commonly used features are:

(a) IF . . . THEN, e.g.
670 IF BETA THEN 240
says if BETA is not zero, then jump to 240.
110 IF MIN < 6 THEN 3230
says if MIN is less than 6, then jump to 3230.

(b) GOSUB . . . RETURN are two instructions for use with sub-routines, e.g. 980 GOSUB 2000
sends control to the subroutine at 2000.
This subroutine must finish with the instruction 2740 RETURN which returns control the calling main program.

(c) All variables in Applesoft Basic are assumed to be floating point unless their names end with "%", e.g. ALPHA %
in which case the variable is treated as an integer value.

(d) Strings are sets of characters and can be handled by assigning them names (like variables), e.g.

300 DESCR\$ = "WATER TEMPERATURE"
310 PRINT DESCR\$
causes WATER TEMPERATURE to be displayed. The dollar sign identifies the label as a string.

(e) Sometimes it is necessary in a Basic program to store a data file on floppy disc or read it back from floppy disc. The commands to DOS to perform these functions are, of course, BSAVE and BLOAD. They are implemented within a Basic program in the following way:
680 "PRINT BLOAD RATIOS"
↑
Press CONTROL and D simultaneously at this point when entering this instruction. This causes the data file RATIOS to be transferred from discette to its appropriate memory location (specified when RATIOS was stored originally).

(f) When a program is fully operational it is useful to produce a hard copy (printer) listing for documentation purposes. To do this ensure that the program is loaded into memory using LOAD or RUN, then:
KEY in PR# 1 and press RETURN,
Press CONTROL and I simultaneously, key in 80N and press RETURN,
Key in LIST and press RETURN,
and program listing will be printed.

(g) Finally some of the remaining Basic commands are:
INPUT — displays a question mark and waits for the operator to key in a number or string.
DATA — creates a list of data items which can be used by READ statements.
READ — when the first READ statement is executed, its first váriable takes on the value of the first element in the DATA list; the second variable takes on the value of the second element in the DATA list; and so on.
SIN, COS, SQR, etc. — sine, cosine, square root and several other trigonometrical and arithmetic functions.

9.2 THE TEXAS 9900 MICROCOMPUTER

9.2.1 The Texas University training board

The Texas 9900 was one of the first 16-bit microcomputers. It is widely used and some of its main applications are in:

(a) Hotpoint washing-machine controllers.

(b) TEC cash registers.

(c) JPM fruit machines.

(d) DVMs.

(e) Programmable logic controllers, etc.

It is produced for training purposes in the form of the TM 990/189 University Board, shown in Figure 9.4. This board contains a 9980A microprocessor, 4 K of ROM, 1 K of RAM and two input/output chips which have a total capacity of forty-four input/output signals. A keyboard is provided for program entry in machine code or assembly language. The input/output devices include LEDs for indication purposes, a loudspeaker and a drive to an audio cassette for program dumping purposes.

9.2.2 The 9980A microprocessor

The special features of this 16-bit microprocessor are that it has only a 16 K addressing range and its 16 registers are any consecutive 16 words in RAM, i.e. it has no accumulator or working registers on-chip. Although this slows down normal program operation it avoids having to store the registers when an interrupt occurs; the interrupting program simply uses a different set of registers in RAM. Additionally all of its registers can be used as accumulators.

Figure 9.5 shows the construction of the CPU and its connections to memory and input/output. Notice the normal features of ALU, Control Unit (fed by Instruction Register), Program Counter and Status Register. The 8-bit latch is necessary with 16-bit microprocessors because memory is always 8-bit. Consequently 2 bytes of memory have to be transferred for each CPU word operation, and these are placed in parallel for the internal 16-bit buses of the CPU.

The novel feature of this particular microprocessor is the use of Workspace Register, which indicates the start address in RAM of the sixteen registers.

The instruction set is shown in Table 9.6. Some instructions are one word (16 bits) long, e.g.

A R3, R4

says add the contents of R3 to R4 and place the answer in R4 (R = Register)

Other instructions are two words long, e.g.

A1 R6, 4

says add 4 to the contents of R6 and place the answer in R6. The number 4 is stored in a second word in the instruction.

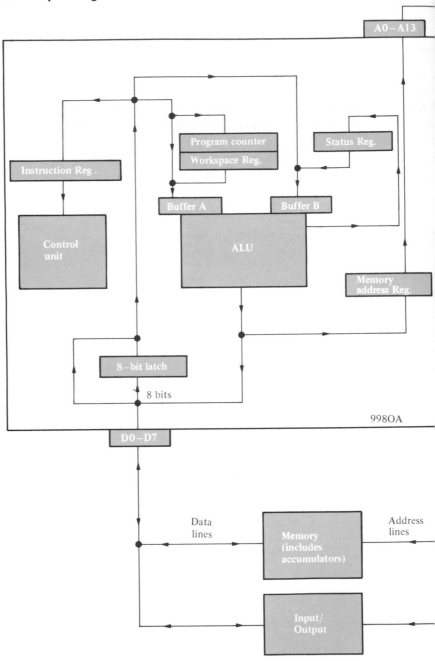

FIGURE 9.5 TEXAS 9980A MICROPROCESSOR

TABLE 9.6 TEXAS 9980 A INSTRUCTION SET

Mnemonic	Meaning	Mnemonic	Meaning
A	Add	JOP	Jump if odd parity
AB	Add bytes	LDCR	Output (to address in R12)
ABS	Absolute value	LI	Load immediate
AI	Add immediate	LIMI	Load interrupt mask
ANDI	AND immediate	LREX	User defined
B	Branch	LWPI	Load workspace pointer
BL	Branch and link		immediate
BLWP	Branch and load workspace	MOV	Move
	pointer	MOVB	Move bytes
C	Compare	MPY	Multiply
CB	Compare bytes	NEG	Negate
CI	Compare immediate	ORI	OR immediate
CKOF	User defined	RSET	Reset
CKON	User defined	RTWP	Return workspace pointer
CLR	Clear operand	S	Subtract
COC	Compare ones corresponding	SB	Subtract bytes
CZC	Compare zeroes	SBO	Output single bit-set to 1
	corresponding		(to address in R12)
DEC	Decrement	SBZ	Output single bit-set to 0
DECT	Decrement by two	SETO	Set to ones
DIV	Divide	SLA	Shift left arithmetic
IDLE	Idle	SOC	Set ones corresponding
INC	Increment	SOCB	Set ones corresponding bytes
INCT	Increment by two	SRA	Shift right arithmetic
INV	Invert	SRC	Shift right circular
JEQ	Jump if equal	SRL	Shift right logical
JGT	Jump if greater than	STCR	Input (from address in R12)
JH	Jump if high	STST	Store status register
JHE	Jump if high or equal	STWP	Store workspace pointer
JL	Jump if low	SWPB	Swap bytes
JLE	Jump if low or equal	SZC	Set zeroes corresponding
JLT	Jump if less than	SZCB	Set zeroes corresponding
JMP	Jump unconditional		bytes
JNC	Jump if no carry	TB	Test bit
JNE	Jump if not equal	X	Execute
JNO	Jump if no overflow	XOP	Extended operation
JOC	Jump if carry	XOR	Exclusive OR

The following addressing modes are available.

(a) <u>DIRECT</u>
   e.g. MOV R1, R4 says move the contents of R1 to R4.

(b) <u>INDIRECT</u>
   e.g. MOV R1, *R4 says move the contents of R1 to the address held in R4.

(c) <u>SYMBOLIC</u>

e.g. MOV R1, @>3F00 says move the contents of R1 to the address 3F00 (>indicates Hex).

(d) <u>IMMEDIATE</u>

e.g. L1 R2, 100 says load R2 with 100.

(e) <u>RELATIVE</u>

This is used with the jump instructions, e.g. JEQ +6 says jump, if status equal bit is 1, 6 words further on (each word is 16 bits).

(f) <u>INDEXED</u>

This is described later in section 9.2.5.

9.2.3 Texas 9901 input/output chips

There are two input/output chips which are available for use with the University board. They each have a capacity of 16+6 = 22 input/output signals. The first chip is totally scheduled for driving the keyboard, numerical display, loudspeaker and cassette drive. Only 4 bits of the other chip are used for LED's, the remaining bits are spare.

Tables 9.7 and 9.8 show the bit assignments and corresponding input/output addresses which have to be set in R2.

TABLE 9.7 IC11 (U11) INPUT/OUTPUT CHIP

TABLE 9.8 IC10 (U10) INPUT/OUTPUT CHIP

R12 address	Identity	R12 address	Identity
420	DIGIT SEL A	20	LED 1
422	B	22	LED 2
424	C	24	LED 3
426	D	26	LED 4
428	SEGMENT A	28	
42A	B	2A	
42C	C	20	
42E	D	2E	
430	E	30	SPARE
432	F	32	
434	G	34	
436	P	36	
438	DISPLAY TRIGGER	38	
43A	SHIFT LED	3A	
43C	LOUDSPEAKER	3C	
43E	CASSETTE WRITE	3E	
	CASSETTE READ	INT 6	
	INT 5	INT 5	SPARE INPUT
	INT 4	INT 4	
	INT 3	INT 3	
	INT 2	INT 2	
	INT 1	INT 1	

The LDCR instruction outputs from the specified register the specified number of bits to the address in R12. For example:

L1 R12, >20
LDCR R4, 10

causes the least significant 10 bits of R4 to be sent to input/output addresses starting at Hex 20. If the number of bits is 0, then all 16 bits are sent.

The other input/output instructions are SB0 and SBZ for output, and STCR and TB for input.

Notice that the 9901 chip has additional features for interval timing and handling interrupts.

9.2.4 The monitor program

When the University Board is switched on and RET is pressed the monitor programme is entered. The following facilities are available from the keyboard:

(a) M0242 RET causes the monitor to display the contents of memory location Hex 0242 (RET is a single key).

If 1234 RET is then keyed in, the Hex number 1234 is entered into 0242.

(b) P causes the monitor to display the contents of the program counter. These can be altered by entering 0220 RET, and the program counter will be set to 0220.

(c) E RET will cause the monitor to run the test program which commences at the address specified by the P command.

E0236 RET will cause the monitor to run the test program as far as the breakpoint at 0236. Control will then be transferred back to monitor when RET is pressed.

(d) R3 RET will cause the monitor to display the contents of Register 3. This is particularly useful after the running of a test program in order to check program operation. Press RET again to return to monitor.

(e) S will cause the monitor to single shot one instruction through a test program.

(f) D200 224 20A IDT NAME Y (IDT is displayed by monitor) causes the contents of memory locations 200 to 224 to be dumped onto audio cassette; 20A is stored as the first instruction in the program, and NAME is the name of the test program. The cassette recorder must be switched to REC and PLAY.

(g) L RET causes the monitor to read off cassette. The cassette recorder must be switched to PLAY.

9.2.5 Texas assembler

The assembler program is called by monitor. The assembler converts assembly language programs into machine code.

To enter the assembler and to start assembly at memory location 0200, enter

A0200 RET

To transfer assembly control to a different memory area, e.g. if it is required to leave space for data in the middle of a program, enter

SP AORG SP > 240 RET (SP is a single key).

and the assembler will assemble the next instruction into Hex 240 (notice that the hex symbol is required here).

Table 9.9 shows the assembly language program and the keyboard entry requirements for the following simple program which adds two numbers and displays the result:

LWP1 > 300 Load workspace pointer (registers start at 300)
L1 R1, 4   Load R1 with 4
L1 R2, 3   Load R2 with 3
A R1, R2   Add R1 to R2, answer in R2
XOP R2, 10   Display R2
XOP R3, 13   Turn on display

It is not necessary to understand the last two instructions, which are subroutine calls on monitor subroutines.

Table 9.9 shows the addresses into which the program is assembled and the machine code which is loaded by the assembler. Notice that the first three instructions are all two words long. The assembler displays the machine code for each instruction entered.

TABLE 9.9 TEXAS PROGRAM EXAMPLE 1:
ADD TWO NUMBERS AND DISPLAY RESULT

Address	Machine code	Keyboard entry
		A0200RET
0200	02E0, 0300	SPLWPISP > 300 RETRETRET
0204	0201, 0004	SPLISPR1, 4 RETRETRET
0208	0202, 0003	SPLISPR2, 3 RETRETRET
020C	A081	SPASP R1, R2RETRET
020E	2E82	SPXOPSPR2, 10RETRET
0210	2F43	SPXOPSPR3, 13RETRET
		SPENDRETRET

If the Add instruction had used indirect addressing the program would have produced the wrong result, i.e. a "bug" would exist, for

A R1, *R2

says add the contents of R1 to the contents of the memory address which is held in R2 (*not* the data held in R2 directly).

A more complicated program which employs loops and input/output features is shown in flowchart form in Figure 9.6. This program illustrates each of 4 LEDs in sequence, with a time delay between each illumination. The keyboard entry procedure and the assembled machine code are shown in Table 9.10.

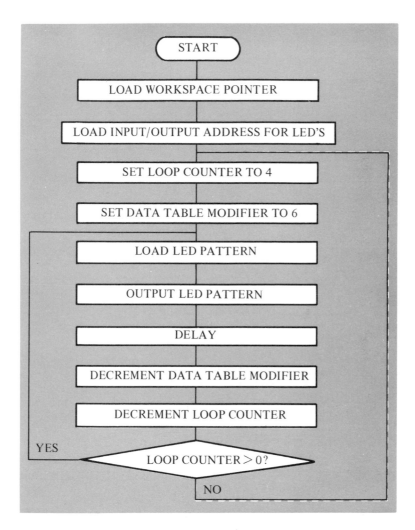

FIGURE 9.6 FLOW CHART FOR TEXAS PROGRAM EXAMPLE 2 —
ILLUMINATED LED'S IN SEQUENCE (WITH DELAY)

The program is as follows:

LWPI > 340   Load workspace pointer
LI R12, > 20   Input/output address of LEDs

ST LI R2, 4	Loop counter
LI R3, 6	Data table modifier
CO MOV @ LE(R3), R4	Fetch LED pattern from data table
LDCR R4, 0	Output LED pattern
LI RO, >7FFF	Delay count
DE DEC RO	Decrement delay count
JGT DE	Jump if delay not finished
DECT R3	Decrement data table modifier (by 2)
DEC R2	Decrement loop count
JGT CO	Jump if loop count positive
JMP ST	Jump to start

TABLE 9.10 TEXAS PROGRAM EXAMPLE 2:
ILLUMINATE LEDs IN SEQUENCE (WITH DELAY)

Address	Machine code	Keyboard entry
		A0200RET
0200		LESPDATASP 1,2,4,8 RET (5 times)
0208	02E0, 0340	SPLWPISP > 340 RETRETRET
020C	020C, 0020	SPLISPR12, > 20 RETRETRET
0210	0202, 0004	STSPLISPR2, 4 RETRETRET
0214	0203, 0006	SPLISPR3, 6 RETRETRET
0218	C123, 0200	COSPMOVSP@LE(R3), R4 RETRETRET
021C	3004	SPLDCRSPR4, 0 RETRET
021E	0200, 7FFF	SPLISPRO, >7FFF RETRETRET
0222	0600	DESPDECSPRO RETRET
0224	15FE	SPJGTSPDE RETRET
0226	0643	SPDECTSPR3 RETRET
0228	0602	SPDECSPR2 RETRET
022A	15F6	SPJGTSPCO RETRET
022C	10F1	SPJMPSPST RETRET
		SPENDRETRET

Table 9.10 shows the assembler command DATA which sets up a 4-value data table which holds the LED patterns to light each LED in turn.

The flow chart shows a single block marked DELAY, which is in fact a simple 3-instruction decrementing delay loop.

The program re-cycles continuously, i.e. the program will sequence through the LEDs for ever.

Notice the use of labels, viz. ST, CO and DE, which enable the assembly language programmer to forget about absolute memory addresses.

The MOV instruction at CO demonstrates the feature of INDEXED addressing. Without R3 in brackets the move operation would transfer the contents of memory address LE to R4. With R3 in brackets the address of LE is modified by the contents of R3 before the instruction is obeyed. For example, on the first run through the main program loop R3 is set to 6, so the move instruction transfers the contents of LE +6 to R4.

To exit from a test program and to return to monitor, operate the LOAD key and press RET.

To abort the assembly of any instruction, press SHIFT X.

FURTHER READING

1. *Applesoft II,* Apple Computer Inc., Cupertino, Cal., U.S.A., 1981.
2. *Microcomputer User's Guide,* TM990/189, Texas Insruments, Inc., Houston, USA, 1979.

Index